Avinash Sai is a writer and book reviewer who launched his Bookstagram account, @bookloafer, six years ago. Since then, he has amassed over 165,000 followers. He published his debut romance novel in 2021, followed by a short story collection in 2023 — both of which received critical acclaim. In his free time, Avinash enjoys watching movies and studying paintings. His mission is to inspire people to read quality books and cultivate lifelong reading habits.

Negative is the New Positive

How Positivity Obsession is Damaging Our Mental Health and How Negative Emotions Help Us Become Whole

Avinash Sai

To my **Peddhamma**, Anantha Lakshmi,

She was the strongest woman I had seen. I wish I could have a bit of her strength and ability to endure hardships. We miss her. Om Shanti.

Table of Contents

Author's Note

This book challenges the popular narrative. Like many aspects of life, we rarely question what we're told. We often surrender ourselves to ideas presented to us, even when they are toxic and drain our souls. This is particularly true when it comes to positivity.

In modern times, we have been led to believe that we can reach a state of paradise simply by thinking positively. We are told that, at our core, we have the potential to adopt a blissful, positive mindset—we just need to tap into it and return to our "default" mood. What's often left unsaid, even after realizing that happiness isn't something we can magically achieve, is that this pursuit isn't an ideal we should strive for.

Positivity, with its firm grip, has infiltrated every part of our lives. At this point, it feels impossible to avoid. To speak against it often brands you as a pessimist. But the truth must be told, regardless of the labels others may place on you. This book is an attempt to speak that truth: we need to embrace all emotions and experiences to be whole and live a meaningful life. We cannot choose an emotion or state and force ourselves into it—it's detrimental to our mental health.

As a reader, you might already be familiar with some of the ideas presented here. I've largely incorporated them to tell a different perspective. I've also included a few concepts I discovered while researching the book, which I believe will be helpful. But more than anything, I've written this book based on what I truly believe and follow wholeheartedly. I'm confident that you will find value in it.

To make this book accessible to everyone, I've kept the language simple, avoiding technical jargon and complex sentences. I've intentionally repeated some facts and insights for emphasis, as I believe this book offers something for everyone.

Because the term "positive" has become so toxic in recent times, I avoid using the phrase "toxic positivity" when discussing it. Since the book explores our obsession with positive emotions, I've also touched on our collective pursuit of happiness. I often use "positivity" and "happiness" interchangeably—if I mention one, it could easily refer to the other.

Part 1

"Life is a process of becoming, a combination of states we have to go through. Where people fail is that they wish to elect a state and remain in it. This is a kind of death" – Anais Nin, an Essayist

1

Positivity, a Modern-day Scam

"The desire for a more positive experience is itself a negative experience. Paradoxically, accepting one's negative experience is, in itself, a positive experience." -Mark Manson, author of *The Subtle Art of Not Giving a F*ck.*

Never in human history have we been so flooded with constant messages of positivity and happiness. They are everywhere: on social media, in movies, YouTube videos, and even in our day-to-day conversations. It's as if we can't go a day without mentioning the word "positive." Scroll through Instagram or Facebook, and you'll come across hundreds—if not thousands—of posts and videos featuring positivity and happiness quotes like, "Be positive," "Happiness is a choice," or "Change your thoughts to be happy," and so on. The messages seem endless.

We've reached a point where we're oversaturated with positivity advice. Rather than easing our nerves, it often makes us feel more anxious, stressed, disappointed, sad, and, in some cases, even depressed. The idea of positivity is so pervasive that it's seeped into nearly every area of our lives. If you're a student, you're expected to maintain a positive mindset; if you're an employee, you're expected to take on extra work, as saying "no" goes against positive workplace culture. If you're a celebrity, sharing your true feelings—especially anything that reveals vulnerability—is often discouraged.

In the shadow of constant positivity, we're losing our authentic selves. Instead of expressing our feelings and emotions, we're suppressing them. The popular notion is to ignore negative feelings and replace them with positive ones. Not only is this counterproductive, but it also makes it harder to face our true emotions. Feelings that are not addressed—or, in other words, suppressed—will eventually rise to the surface, creating further discomfort and often leading to immature reactions. As psychologist Dr. Emily Will Broth says, "Unpleasant feelings are part of the human experience."[1] To be human is to experience the full range of emotions.

Looking back through history, our ancestors spent most of their time plowing fields, growing crops, and gathering the harvest. They had little time to sit and ponder; thinking was largely reserved for elites, particularly philosophers. These thinkers, of course, pondered happiness and what makes us truly happy. Philosophers from East to West shared their insights. Socrates, the Greek philosopher, said, "Happiness is already there. It is within us. We have just forgotten about it and need to remember it again." Lao Tzu, an ancient Chinese philosopher, advised, "Be content with what you have; rejoice in the way things are. When you realize there is nothing lacking, the whole world belongs to you." Most of this advice was harmless and, to some extent, genuinely helpful, emphasizing being present, living by virtues, and expecting nothing in return.

Since the early 20th century, everything has changed. People flocked to cities where opportunities were abundant. We began working in jobs that were less labor-intensive and offered stability, security, food, and shelter. Our quality of life improved, with access to clean drinking water, better housing, and easier access to education. Meanwhile, universities began studying happiness scientifically. Despite wars and periods of unrest, most countries eventually gained independence and experienced prosperity and development. Among the most significant changes was increased access to books.

Previously, education and book ownership were privileges enjoyed mainly by the elite. But as printing became cheaper and education became more accessible, people began reading books beyond their religious texts. This era saw a surge in the publication and worldwide sales of self-help books. Two books that popularized the idea that you can change your life by changing your thoughts were THINK

AND GROW RICH BY NAPOLEON HILL AND THE POWER OF POSITIVE THINKING BY NORMAN VINCENT PEALE.

In Think and Grow Rich, the author explains how you can achieve success by feeding your subconscious mind with the right words and thoughts. While it's essential to stay focused on our goals, factors like environment and culture also play a major role in shaping what we can achieve. Similarly, in The Power of Positive Thinking, the author emphasizes positive thinking as a pathway to success, problem-solving, and overall happiness. Looking at the bright side might help ease your nerves in the moment, but positive thinking alone is not a solution for everything.

These early books didn't create the modern trends of toxic positivity, but they paved the way for it in the years that followed. Self-help gurus, spiritual speakers, mentors, and coaches began appearing in great numbers. They started publishing books on solutions to complex problems, promoting positive attitudes, teaching how to think positively, how to avoid negative thoughts, how to be happy, how not to be sad, and so on. According to the Internet Archive's Open Library, there are over 109,350 titles containing the word "Happiness," with the majority being self-help books. Likewise, in the ISBN database— the world's largest book database—there are over 10,000 titles that include the word "Positive." Clearly, the trend toward positivity has been on the rise since the 1950s.

But why are there so many books on the same topic? If happiness could be achieved by following ten simple steps, would we really need thousands of books that essentially say the same thing? If positivity is as easy as thinking positively, wouldn't one book suffice? Fundamentally, people seek quick fixes for complex problems. While reading these books might offer temporary relief, sooner or later, we often fall back into the same routines and thought patterns, encouraging us to reach for yet another book on positivity or happiness.

Self-help gurus and coaches capitalize on this desperation by selling courses, workshops, and tutorials, all promising that by the end, you'll be miraculously positive or happy. But in reality, it's unlikely that any course will provide a lasting solution.

The truth is, pain and suffering are inevitable parts of life. There is nothing wrong with feeling happy or good, of course. But the problem arises when we expect to feel happy or positive all the time. We'll discuss this further in Chapter 2. For now, it's worth recognizing that these self-help pundits and so-called life coaches are ultimately selling hope—the hope that you can achieve happiness and positivity simply by thinking a certain way. Their books primarily focus on convincing you that they have the answers you're looking for.

Take a closer look at these gurus, and you'll often find that they enjoy lavish mansions and luxurious lifestyles. They seem to have everything they want, able to summon anything at the snap of their fingers, while they preach happiness and positivity to us. It's widely believed that money can't buy happiness, and many people agree. I used to agree, too, until a psychologist-turned-professor told me that while money may not buy happiness, it is essential for it. Ryan Holiday, author of Ego is the Enemy, echoes this sentiment. In his book Discipline is Destiny, he states, "Money doesn't buy happiness, but it can buy you out of some frustrations."

You and I are different. Our circumstances are different. We are not privileged. We have to work hard just to get by. Life isn't always fair. Job insecurity, financial pressures, and family responsibilities create stress and anxiety. When we hear a celebrity like Jennifer Aniston, who played Rachel on F.R.I.E.N.D.S, say, "You can undo a lot of things. If you're not happy, you can become happy. Happiness is a choice. That's the thing I really feel," or when a spiritual leader like the Dalai Lama says, "The purpose of our lives is to be happy," we feel excluded. We wonder, if they can do it, why can't we? Burdened by the struggles of daily life, we long for happiness and positivity. After all, who wouldn't want to be free of negative thoughts and live a fulfilling life?

However, we are missing the point. Instead of focusing solely on the pursuit of happiness or positivity, we should be developing emotional competence—the ability to navigate our emotions with minimal distress. Emotional competence enables us to recognize, understand, and express our feelings effectively. We will delve deeper into emotional competence in Chapter 8. In the next chapter, we'll explore the toxic effects of positivity and how it can be detrimental to our well-being.

Signs That You Are Burdened by Positivity

You try to hide your true feelings.

You feel minimized by "feel-good" quotes or statements.

You struggle to accept or acknowledge your emotions.

You feel ashamed to express frustration or anything other than positivity.[2]

Questions to Ask Yourself:

Do you push yourself to be happy and positive all the time?

How do you handle negative emotions? Do you allow yourself to sit with them, or do you suppress them?

Do you feel pressure to be positive at all times?

Do you believe emotions exist for a reason?

When was the last time you felt an intense emotion? How did you calm yourself down?

2

How Positivity Obsession Ruining Your Life

"Trying to force a positive view is like trying to cover up a stain with a bright cloth. The stain remains. It's only by embracing the messiness that we find true resilience."
— Pema Chödrön, *a Tibetan Buddhist*

What's wrong with wishing for positivity and happiness in life? Nothing, of course. After all, we face financial stress, work with difficult people, and constantly worry about the future. There are countless things that consume our thoughts every day. Life can be hard, and the only truly satisfying moment may be when we finally fall into bed after an exhausting day. Everyday routines often drain the joy from life. Without joy, we're merely existing.

So, when we encounter positivity, it can feel like stumbling upon treasure. Positivity seems harmless, especially because we believe it can ease our worries and make us happy. We start to think it's something we should embrace wholeheartedly, following it religiously. We turn to books on positivity and happiness, practice positive thinking, and visualize good things happening to us. We even buy journals that promise to bring out the best in ourselves. But after a while, the initial results we experienced begin to fade.

This is where self-hate thoughts arise. We want to be positive, but we fail while trying to do so. But many people are oblivious to the fact that we cannot simply choose a state of mind and be in it indefinitely. We start to blame ourselves for failing to keep ourselves positive. According to Gillian Fagan, a therapist, "Too much positivity can reinforce feelings of failure when life doesn't go the way we want" [1] We often feel we are falling behind as people we admire seem to always be succeeding.

The truth is, we don't know what truly happens in most people's lives. We see a fraction, specifically what they choose to show on social media. Our standards should always be set by comparing ourselves to our past selves but not with others—especially self-help gurus. Their livelihoods depend on selling a vision. Naturally, they present themselves as positive, even if they are not always feeling that way.

It's time to recognize that positivity has its limitations. Emotions and feelings serve a purpose, even the negative ones. They convey messages that we need to understand and interpret. Psychologist Alder Hal E . Hartfield expresses this well, stating, "One of the primary reasons we have emotions in the first place is to help us evaluate our experiences." [2]

If we, however, place too much emphasis on positivity, not only do we become more emotionally vulnerable when difficulties arise, but we also miss opportunities for growth. According to research, the most meaningful experiences are often painful. [3] By fixating on one emotion, we may hold ourselves back from learning valuable lessons and gaining wisdom.

If you are frustrated with trying to maintain positivity, you're not alone. There is no denying that positivity works for some people, particularly those with upbeat and outgoing personalities who have little to no stress. However, for others, it does more harm than good. Before we delve into the importance of pain and suffering, we need to address the toxic aspects and effects of modern-day positivity.

Positivity Cult

It would be an understatement to say that the positivity movement now has a cult-like following. Cult members may include ordinary people, like friends and family.

However, more often than not, these members occupy superior positions and preach positivity for a living—spiritual gurus, self-help experts, and life coaches, for example. As we know, it all starts with a promise, or more precisely, a hope. These figures present their ideology and principles. They suggest that subscribing to their teachings will lead to happiness and positivity. But if you question their ideas, you risk being labeled as a negative thinker or pessimist.

To join the cult, the principles are simple:

Are you sad? Be positive, it could have been worse.

Feeling low? Be positive, and look on the bright side.

Angry? Be positive, life is short.

Going through heartbreak? Be positive, everything will be alright.

Broke? Be positive, at least you're alive.

Feeling hopeless? Be positive, God will take care of everything.

Got fired? Be positive, everything happens for a reason. [4]

On the surface, this type of advice seems harmless and even helpful. But the devil is in the details. When you look closely, you'll see that it minimizes your negative emotions and feelings, encouraging you to ignore them rather than sit with them and understand why they're there in the first place. Members of the positivity cult urge you to deny your negative emotions as if they don't exist. In doing so, you not only become emotionally numb, but you may also feel more agitated and helpless.

Unaddressed emotions can cause havoc later. The cult prescribes positivity for every situation, regardless of how you're feeling, leaving no room for self-reflection. For example, if you're fired, simply believing that "everything happens for a reason" instead of examining why it happened may lead to a similar situation in the future. This creates a vicious cycle.

According to Martin E. P. Seligman, an American psychologist, optimism can sometimes prevent us from seeing reality with the necessary clarity.[5] Lessons must be learned; otherwise, we'll keep making the same mistakes and paying a hefty price each time. Remember, **the discomfort of addressing your tough emotions in the moment is far better than facing the damage they may cause later on.**

Positivity Suppresses Your Emotions and Feelings

Emotions and feelings provide valuable insights into our internal state. By tuning into and listening to them, we can often calm ourselves and even uncover opportunities for growth. When we focus solely on positive emotions and deny all negative ones, we set ourselves up for misery. As Tony Rodriguez, a journalist and psychotherapist, explains, "Attempting to suppress [negative] thoughts can backfire and even diminish our sense of contentment."[6] Many psychological and physiological studies have concluded that "pretending to be okay increases internal stress. Hiding feelings of anger and sadness can lead to depression, anxiety, and even physical illness."[7]

Even though we may notice frustration and anger building up after suppressing negative thoughts, we rarely address it. This is because we often aren't aware that hiding these true feelings causes irritation and frustration in the first place. Since positivity has become the ultimate goal, we tend to accept ongoing distress rather than addressing the source.

Humans naturally fear facing difficult emotions. We often go to great lengths to avoid pain. But as psychotherapist Gillian Fagan noted, "avoiding pain is, in a way, a form of pain."[8] We can't simply erase emotions or thoughts; that's not how the mind works. The more we try to suppress negative thoughts, the more they haunt us. Carl Jung, a renowned psychotherapist, aptly said, "What you resist persists." Unaddressed emotions can affect our daily moods, while negative emotions can actually help us connect with others and foster transformation. Studies show that personal crises and losses often lead to profound growth.[9]

Pressure to be Positive

I was 17 years old when I started taking reading seriously. Like many others, I began with popular self-help books. I would take notes and try to apply the concepts in any way I could. In nearly every book I read, the idea of positivity was touched upon in some form—whether it was developing a positive attitude, practicing positive thinking, using positive visualization, or cultivating a positive mindset. Alongside this, many authors discussed the successful habits of millionaires and billionaires, and, as you might have guessed, positivity was always mentioned.

I was swept away by the belief, widely popularized by self-help books, that you could achieve anything by simply thinking positively. I began to implement these ideas, but soon enough, I was disappointed.

By that time, the positivity movement had already infiltrated academia and the workplace, and it was even included in school curricula. My college offered a course on personal development, which covered the importance of a positive mindset. However, it was difficult for me to maintain positivity all the time. I felt like I was falling short. It often felt like I was the odd one out. While others likely had the same struggles, it seemed taboo to speak the truth out loud.

You have to exert a lot of energy to maintain a certain emotional state. It doesn't come naturally—and it's not sustainable either. It's draining, to say the least, and it definitely takes a toll on mental health. Eventually, I gave up on the pursuit of constant positivity. As I delved deeper into books on human nature, psychology, trauma, and biology, it became clear to me that positivity shouldn't be taken too seriously. It's not an ideal we should strive for. Societal pressures persist, and many people surrender to them, eventually burning themselves out emotionally in the process.

Positivity Doesn't Let Us Embrace Ourselves

Every human being is different. Although we all have basic human emotions and facial expressions, how we react and how intensely we feel an emotion varies. This could be due to our genetic makeup (also, epigenetics passed down by our parents), the culture or environment we were born into, the type of parenting we received, our childhood experiences, the trauma we've endured, the habits we've developed, and even the books we've read.

As there is no single way to live life, there is no single, standard way we should respond to our circumstances. Everyone responds in the way they know, shaped by their life experiences.

Given such a unique composition, it's foolish to expect others to feel or express emotions in the same way you do. Some of us struggle with anxiety, others may be prone to sadness, and many are battling addiction. It's not their fault for being the way they are. In fact, they are likely doing everything they can to be "normal." But an obsession with positivity makes it incredibly difficult to accept and be content with ourselves. As we strive to reach an idealized version of ourselves, we often abandon our true, authentic selves. How we feel is uniquely ours.

Often what people consider weaknesses are actually strengths in disguise. Evolutionary psychologists Paul W. Andrews and J. Anderson Thomson argue that "sadness brings cognitive benefits." Studies have shown that "sadness makes us better at assessing reality and social situations." Not only that, but "sadness can even make us more productive at work by enhancing focus and helping us learn from mistakes."[10]

We need to learn not to beat ourselves up. We have to accept who we are. That's when we can see real change.

Positivity Stuns Growth

At every point in life, there are opportunities for growth. Although Phil Knight, founder of Nike, says opportunities rarely appear in the form you expect, they almost always involve pain, heartbreaks, low phases, setbacks, and failures. If we are sitting down with ourselves and introspecting, we get insights into what we are doing wrong and what we should do when we face the same situation again. But if you always want to stay positive, you are missing out on the chances to grow.

According to Helen Dillon, a therapist, "being positive all the time means there is no critical analysis taking place or taking stock of one's current situation." [11] In other words, an obsession with positivity shuts down our critical thinking skills. Without complete awareness of where we are and where we need to go, is like nailing our coffin. Instead of pushing ourselves to deal with what's happening, we are being blindsided to remain positive no matter what the situation is.

For you to grow in life, you have to face your obstacles, including your emotions, feelings, and thoughts. Hard times reveal strength in our character. It is only through discomfort that we get emotionally mature. Remember that wisdom can only be attained through experiencing suffering and loss. There is no other way around it.

Positivity Keeps Us in Illusion

When we want to be positive all the time, we are casting an illusion upon ourselves. It feels good as long as we don't face any negative experiences. Once the shit hits the fan, we don't know where to turn. Because we have been wishing life to go as we want. It has been studied that "people who place a higher value on positivity or happiness all the time, they tend to react poorly to their negative emotions."[12] Clearly, positive forecasting will not go well for individuals who want to be positive.

Optimism has its drawbacks. Often "unrealistic optimism neglects the threats altogether."[13] In a culture that places high regard on positive emotions, it fails to appreciate how beneficial our negative emotions usually are. We generally disregard pessimists by labeling them as negative thinkers. But not according to psychologists Martin E. P. Seligman and Dereck Isaacowitz. In their study, they found "pessimists were less prone to depression than optimists after experiencing negative life events, such as losing a loved one."[14] It can be traced back to preparing for worst-case scenarios.

Our lives would be much smoother if we accepted situations and events that happen as they are rather than wishing them to happen as we want them to. It gives us the courage to confront our thoughts, further developing our emotional resilience. But we have to give up the standards such as I MUST feel this way or I SHOULD feel this way. When we come out of illusions, life becomes much more breathable and livable.

A Word on Positive Affirmations

The question is do affirmations work? Yes and No. It works for people who have high self-esteem and an outgoing personality. Reading out affirmations might improve their mood and help them go through the day. However, affirmations can be disastrous for people who have low self-esteem. Not only do they fail, but they cause frustration as well.[15] Forcing yourself to be something that you clearly are not, creates the gap where self-doubt prevails. If they are not working, ditching them is the best solution.

An interesting fact:

It is generally believed that positive emotions improve our performance. According to an observational study, a patient is more likely to die if the surgery is taking place on the surgeon's birthday. What an irony! [16]

3

Not Happiness. Meaning is Important

"The purpose of life is not to be happy. It is to be useful, honorable, compassionate, and have it make some difference that you have lived and lived well" – Ralph Waldo Emerson,
an American philosopher.

Many of us are not true sufferers. However, it is undeniable that every person's suffering is unique, as is their individual experience. One should acknowledge that modern life provides comforts that our ancestors could only have fantasized about. Gone are the days of starvation, fear of death, anxiety over invasions, concerns about shelter, and the constant worry of diseases. In the 21st century, most of us are well-fed (in fact, many of us are over-fed), have access to medicine and hospitals, stable sources of income, strong governments to protect us from enemies, and all the amenities needed to thrive and prosper in life. It is a far cry from life just 80 years ago.

A boy was born in 1905 into a secure Jewish family in Vienna, Austria. His life was normal until World War I.

Suddenly, there was no food on his plate. At a young age, he and his siblings went from farm to farm, begging for food. But that did not deter his spirit. By the time he was in high school, he began studying psychology and philosophy. Even before his graduation, he gave a speech on "The Meaning of Life."

Sigmund Freud, the Austrian neurologist, was impressed by the paper when the boy sent it to him. In his reply, Freud asked if he could publish the paper. The boy was astonished. His idol not only replied to his letter but also expressed interest in publishing it. Later, he went on to study medicine, while simultaneously developing his theories and putting them into practice. However, he noticed a peculiar phenomenon: when high school grades were announced, there was a rise in student suicides. To prevent this, he began counseling students. Surprisingly, the following year's suicide rate dropped to zero.

Impressed with the results, he was later appointed head of the Vienna Psychiatric Hospital's Female Suicide Prevention Program, where he saved thousands of women on the verge of taking their own lives. However, dark clouds that had long loomed over Europe soon engulfed Austria. With the Nazi invasion, his private clinic was forced to shut down, and he was restricted to treating only Jewish patients. In 1942, the inevitable occurred. His family, including his newly married wife, were arrested and sent to concentration camps by the Nazis.

Within six months of capture, his father passed away. As if that pain wasn't enough, he and his mother were later ordered to Auschwitz. But his wife was sent to another camp, where she would soon be killed. After arriving at Auschwitz, the two were ordered to stand in one of two lines. Defying the command, he jumped to the line next to him. It was only after reaching the shed that he learned the line they had been forced into initially was the one that led directly to the gas chamber. He barely escaped, but his mother did not. Now, his real ordeal awaited him.

It was easy—and remarkably normal—to lose hope once you were in a concentration camp. You had no idea whether you would be released or killed. Death offered instant liberation from suffering and pain, but it was living that felt like hell. There was never enough food to fill your stomach. You were forced into backbreaking manual labor. You were beaten, tortured, and if you were a woman, sexually assaulted. By the end of the day, you would collapse from the mental and physical exhaustion you endured.

You shouldn't forget that loneliness will consume you as you are stripped of social connections. You won't know if you'll ever see your loved ones again. There's no way to communicate with them, no way to know if they're alive, or if they know you are. This realization will eat you alive.

Death constantly looms over you. If you don't follow orders, they shoot you. If you're accidentally injured, they shoot you. If you get into a fight with another inmate, they shoot you. If you try to escape, they shoot you. If you're not productive enough, they shoot you. If you fall behind, they shoot you. Imagine being fed only a morsel of food and still being expected to meet cruel standards.

But there's no point in committing suicide either. They sent you here to kill you anyway. Sooner or later, you'll be killed or die of starvation. You know you're waiting for death, but you don't know when it will come. Whatever glimmer of hope you had evaporates after a few months. **Courage surrenders to the atrocities you witness.** Living becomes pointless. You become a walking corpse.

The horrors you witness etch themselves deeply into your mind. Often, you're asked to bury the person who arrived with you. A single glance at the burial ground sends a shiver down your spine. You might be lucky enough to survive, but fear and horror grip you to the point of suffocation. At this point, you may wonder, what's the point of living after release? You've seen enough to be haunted by nightmares for the rest of your life.

Yet, one man saw it differently. Though he witnessed the beatings of his comrades, endured physical and mental torture, suffered loneliness, and faced extreme hunger, he emerged from the concentration camps with hope and purpose. He believed that suffering and pain hold meaning. He believed that how we handle our darkest moments reveals who we truly are. That man is Viktor E. Frankl, a psychologist and the author of the life-changing book Man's Search for Meaning.

You Cannot Escape

Pain and suffering are integral parts of life. Contrary to what spiritual gurus often say, **suffering is not optional; it is not a choice. You suffer because you have responsibilities toward life and its happenings. You suffer because you care. Believing it's a choice suggests you don't fully take responsibility for what you love and value.**

After Viktor Frankl was freed from the concentration camp, he observed people who he described as "spiritually bombed out." Years of war and hardship had crushed their souls. He saw that people were "intellectually and culturally starved," [1] many with no direction or idea of how to lead their lives. Brutal experiences can take away the hope to live, and for those who have lost everything, including their loved ones, it becomes difficult to find the courage to wake up each day and go about daily tasks. In response to this disorientation, he began giving speeches and teaching courses on suicide prevention, coping with physical illnesses, and, most importantly, rebuilding life after concentration camps.

Viktor Frankl went on to develop Logotherapy, which guides people in finding meaning in their lives. He argues that **one shouldn't seek happiness, as it doesn't provide a sense of purpose, nor should one chase pleasure, as it lacks meaning.** He observed that those who could endure the horrors and fight to the very end were those who believed they could contribute something through their lives, whether through work or love. In other words, they had a sense of meaning and purpose. It is precisely these two elements that make suffering bearable.

As Friedrich Nietzsche said, "He who knows why can bear any how." If a person understands why they are living, they can face any situation—either by changing it or by adapting to it. That why, the meaning behind your existence, helps you see the long term and look forward to the next day.

Suffering has meaning too if you look for it. In a letter to his friends Wilhelm and Stepha Borner, Viktor Frankl wrote, "Increasingly, I realize that life is so infinitely meaningful that even in suffering and even in failure there still has to be a meaning."[2] Instead of complaining about inconveniences, consider what you can make of the situation, because, as he put it, **"the human soul also appears to be strengthened by experiencing a burden."**[3] Out of suffering emerge the strongest and bravest souls, as Viktor Frankl himself demonstrated.

Of course, suffering is no pleasure. But if you ask someone who has experienced suffering how they would be without it, they would likely say they wouldn't be the same. When we suffer, our character transforms. As Jensen Huang, co-founder and CEO of Nvidia, says, "You want greatness out of them [young entrepreneurs] and greatness is not intelligence. Greatness comes from character. It's formed out of people who suffered." Through suffering, we explore different sides of ourselves we didn't know existed. **When life throws challenges at us, how we react and respond becomes the answer we give back to life.**

Cultivate Meaning

Viktor Frankl outlined three ways through which a person can cultivate meaning and purpose in life. With a sense of purpose, contentment follows. Even on our hardest days, simply reminding ourselves why we are here can calm our nerves and build the strength needed to face our struggles.

Work

Create art—whether it's writing a book, painting, or pursuing something else you love. Whatever form it takes, it should feel as though your work will surpass your "self" and leave a lasting impact. One of the key things that kept Viktor Frankl alive was his desire to publish a book after his release from the camp. Whenever he felt overwhelmed by hopeless thoughts, he would distract himself by imagining he was giving a lecture in an auditorium, sharing the psychological insights he gained from his imprisonment.

Art is an expression of who we are. It allows us to transcend into realms of deeper meaning. The key is to immerse yourself in your work and find purpose in doing so. Many of us may be in jobs that feel easily replaceable, but we need them to survive. This doesn't mean we have to quit. Instead, we can spend our free time doing what makes us feel alive. Frequency and progress don't matter as long as we don't give up.

Love

We often take nature for granted, as if it were our birthright. While we know the harm we're causing, we rarely appreciate nature wholeheartedly. Living in a concrete jungle, greenery has become a rare sight—trees planted here and there, often only as part of Corporate Social Responsibility (CSR) initiatives. But nature is part of us; we belong to the ecosystem. For millions of years, we lived in harmony with nature, while cities are a recent development. Research shows that simply taking a walk in nature relieves stress and calms the mind,[4] and even looking at trees can ease overwhelming thoughts. Make time for nature every week—take a hike, go camping, immerse yourself fully.

Jean-Paul Sartre famously said, **"Hell is other people."** If we're not surrounded by supportive, honest, and kind people, we are likely causing ourselves unnecessary pain. Truthfully, we are social beings; without connections, there's an emotional void that solitude can't fill. This doesn't mean we need to be friends with everyone. Quality matters more than quantity. Being around people who don't align with us can feel lonelier than being alone. It's essential to build meaningful relationships with those who appreciate our presence and stand by us, no matter what we're going through.

Art Overpowers Us

We often see ourselves as the center of the universe, forgetting how small we are within the vast scheme of things. Great art has the power to sweep you off your feet. When you experience a remarkable work—whether a sculpture, painting or any other form—you're completely captivated by its magical presence, losing yourself in the moment. That's the effect of truly great art. **Appreciating human creativity offers profound satisfaction and serves as a reminder of the beauty we often overlook.**

How to View the World

We are all bound by fate, and more often than not, we become victims of its workings. Life isn't fair to many of us. Even when we make no faulty decisions, the people and circumstances around us can make life feel like a living hell. There seems to be no end to human drama or societal pressures. We often feel as if we're walking on a hot pan.

But there is an antidote—it's about shifting how we view things. As Viktor E. Frankl writes in Man's Search for Meaning, "When we are no longer able to change a situation, we are challenged to change ourselves." Change doesn't mean abandoning responsibility; it's about understanding the situation and finding meaning in it. When Frankl was in the concentration camp, he focused on what he would do after his release—publishing his book and sharing his experiences. This vision helped him endure his suffering.

Frankl also believed that long-term thinking makes enduring hardship easier than short-term thinking. He observed that prisoners who fixated on a specific release date—such as Christmas—were often more disappointed and less hopeful when it didn't happen. In contrast, those like Frankl, who held onto hope that they would be released "one day," were more resilient through their misery.

Life will be difficult. It may even get harder in the future. However, we should remember Frankl's words: "Everything can be taken from a man but one thing: the last of the human freedoms—to choose one's attitude in any given set of circumstances, to choose one's own way." By molding ourselves to fit the situation, life becomes less burdensome and more livable.

We can't truly imagine the horrors Frankl and his fellow prisoners endured. We can only read or hear their stories, but we can never fully understand how it felt to be in their shoes. Despite everything, they survived. They endured through hope and a desire to contribute to the world. One last lesson from Viktor Frankl is that happiness shouldn't be pursued directly. As he says, "Happiness cannot be pursued; it must ensue." Simply put, **happiness comes as a by-product of working toward something greater than oneself.**[5]

4

A Refreshing Look at Unwanted Things

"Our painful experiences aren't a liability—
they're a gift. They give us perspective and
meaning, an opportunity to find our unique
purpose and our strength." – Edith Eger,
author of *The Choice.*

We are willing to pay a million dollars to avoid certain things, especially those that are painful and challenge our sense of self-worth. We would do almost anything to erase the traces of our mistakes and experiences that continue to haunt us. However, these experiences are, in fact, essential for our character development and for instilling meaning in our otherwise tedious lives. Instead of trying to rid ourselves of them completely, we should embrace them openly and learn from them. We need to look at them with fresh eyes and recognize that they are also a part of life.

Humans have Regrets

If you ask people how they want to live, they often reply that they want a life without regrets. Regrets are powerful; they stir up intense and distressing emotions. They paralyze us in the moment, making us overthink. When you recall your regrets, you often say to yourself, "I should have done that," "I should've said that," "I should've been more careful," or "I should have had the courage to speak up." These thoughts consume our minds. Because regrets hurt us, we try—or at least wish—to avoid them.

But there's another side to the coin. Although regrets cause emotional pain, they can be incredible sources of growth and provide deep meaning that enriches us. One thing to remember is that, for the most part, we don't create regrets by choice. We make a decision in the moment that later becomes a regret. Perhaps that choice seemed plausible at the time; only afterward do we see its consequences. If the results are what we desired, we feel satisfied. If not, they haunt us for years to come.

How we perceive regrets reveals a great deal about ourselves. If you view them as "opportunities," you'll experience less emotional turmoil and be open to learning the lessons they offer. But if you see them as "threats," you may struggle to stand up for yourself and hesitate to make bold decisions—actions that often lead to self-discovery and realizing your potential. Accepting what happened and thinking about the next course of action, considering our previous choices, helps us move forward. Daniel Pink, author of The Power of Regret, says, "Regret makes us human. Regret makes us better."

How Negative Emotions Fuel Creative Works

It is widely believed that creative people are unusual, perhaps even sad or depressed. If you examine their lives, this belief often appears true. Leo Tolstoy, the renowned Russian writer of War and Peace, and Anna Karenina, lived a turbulent life—his marriage was a disaster. Vincent van Gogh, the Dutch painter famous for The Starry Night, died by shooting himself in the chest. Johann Wolfgang von Goethe, the German writer, published a semi-autobiographical work inspired by his unfulfilled love for a woman. What do these stories imply?

We can channel our melancholy, pain, and longings into art. Susan Cain, author of Quiet and Bittersweet, says, **"Whatever pain you can't get rid of, make it your creative offering."** Emotions like melancholy can fuel the creative process. Sadness brings us closer to reality, and negative emotions bring us closer to ourselves. Instead of trying to eliminate or suppress these feelings, we can use them to create works that bond humanity together.

Poets and writers have been drawing on longing for ages. Longings stir profound emotions within us. We long for things we've lost, things we desire, and things that don't exist. If we can express our longings, we can connect with our fellow humans—because longings are universal.

Sometimes You Need to Give Up

Popular advice tells us, "Don't quit." You've likely seen or heard many success stories where someone didn't give up on their goals and ultimately succeeded. But that's a trap. We only hear about successful outcomes and get swept up by them. In reality, most people quit and pursue other goals—not because they lack determination or discipline, but because they no longer see the results they hoped for.

When we start something, we often believe we should stick with it until it works. If we quit, it feels like a sign of failure. But as Anne Duke, author of Quit, points out, "If you quit something that's no longer worth pursuing, that's not a failure. That's a success." She continues, "Success means following a good decision-making process, not finishing a line, especially if it is the wrong one to cross." Focus on the process, not just the result. If it's not working, let it go and move on to something else.

You Are Not Your Mistakes

The mistakes we make often reveal our deep insecurities and suggest that we're somehow flawed. But mistakes happen as a result of our decisions, not because we're inherently faulty. As humans, we tend to fixate on the end result and blame ourselves when things don't turn out as expected. We need to understand that mistakes are essential for growth. They reveal blind spots in our thinking and decision-making process.

It's true that some mistakes are costly, leaving marks on our character. We might repeatedly think, "I wish I'd known better." But that's not how mistakes work. We make assumptions about outcomes, and it's only when we act on them that we find out if they're accurate. When they're not, mistakes happen. Instead of blaming ourselves, we can use these experiences to improve our decision-making skills.

Edith Eger, a Holocaust survivor and author of The Choice, puts it well: "The truth is we will have unpleasant experiences in our lives, we will make mistakes, we won't always get what we wanted. This is part of being human. The problem – the foundation of persistent suffering – is the belief that discomfort, mistakes, and disappointment signal something about our worth." Self-acceptance is the key.

Let Your Children Have Negative Experiences

We live in a society where children are often overprotected and shielded from challenges, threats, and discomfort. While it's natural for parents to want to protect their children from hurt and disappointment, letting them experience life as it is can be invaluable. Exposure to real-life situations helps children understand reality and shape themselves accordingly. **The today's experiences set expectations for tomorrow.**

When children are overly protected, they become weak and fragile. In nature, a young tree must endure strong winds, which strengthen its trunk and branches and encourage its roots to grow deeper. Without these winds, a tree remains vulnerable, easily uprooted by strong gusts when weather changes. Similarly, children need early challenges to help them become grounded and resilient.

Overindulgent and overly protective parenting can leave children emotionally exposed. They come to expect that the outside world will cater to them as their parents have, and when those expectations aren't met, they may feel vulnerable and easily triggered. Parents may struggle to understand why their children react this way.

By preventing children from facing hardship, pain, failure, and loss, we deprive them of the tools needed for maturity, empathy, and self-acceptance. These experiences are essential for building character. Social psychologist Brock Bastian, in his book The Other Side of Happiness, notes, "Negative experiences provide a valuable pathway to develop resilience." Facing challenging situations teaches us to respond less emotionally when similar events occur again.

Children also need the space to discover their own potential and talents. **One of the worst things a parent can do is deny a child the room to explore who they are.** We shouldn't raise a "snowflake."

Part 2

"All of humanity's problems stem from our inability to sit quietly in a room alone"
- Blaise Pascal, A French Philosopher

5

The Laws of Becoming Whole

"To live fully is to live with an awareness of the rumble of terror that underlies everything" – Ernest Becker, author of *The Denial of Death*

Death unnerves us at our core. The thought of not seeing another day brings a deep discomfort. We avoid reminders of life's brevity; if someone raises the topic of death, we instinctively try to change the subject. Sitting with the unpleasant feelings it brings is challenging. We long to live forever, yet we're acutely aware that our time is limited.

Human life is magical. We witness the world's beauty and its wonders. We fall in love, form strong, rewarding relationships, and find deep fulfillment in these connections, which give us reason to welcome each new sunrise. We forge deep bonds with the places and things we grow up around. So, when we realize that we'll one day lose it all, it's hard to accept.

Our desperation to extend our lives—often beyond human limits—creates opportunities for cunning people to take advantage. Coaches, doctors, and nutrition experts offer longevity products: specialized diets, supplements, medicines, and sometimes unconventional, even dangerous, practices. All these stems from our unquenchable desire to live longer.

There's nothing wrong with wishing for a long, healthy life. After all, nobody wants a body riddled with disease. A healthy life supports productivity, strong bonds, and overall well-being. We should all strive for a lifestyle that includes nutritious food and physical activity, as these alone address most of the health challenges we face now and in the future.

But the question remains: why do we want to live so long? If we make the most of our capacities and the time given to us, why do we feel the need to live beyond 100 years? Our craving for a longer life often comes from our desires. The problem with desires is that once we start fulfilling them, even more desires appear. This is where restlessness and awareness of unrealized goals settle in, driving us to do whatever we can to live forever.

Perhaps not every desire needs to be fulfilled. We can focus on a few that bring us the greatest satisfaction and allow us to leave a meaningful mark on the world. By embracing life's brevity, we can enhance its quality. Remembering how brief our time truly is can help us live to the fullest. It's not complicated—we simply need to start at a place we often avoid and find uncomfortable: the remembrance of our own mortality.

The Law of Meditation of Death

I'm sure some of us have already heard of this concept. A few of us who are avid readers may have read about it and know what it's about. But it's worth revisiting regularly—a piece of advice that could deepen our connection to reality: Memento Mori.

Memento Mori comes from ancient Stoic philosophy. It means "Remember that you are going to die." Every day, upon waking, we should remind ourselves of this. It's a reminder that we are inching closer to our death. It also serves as a cue that we are aging—our energy may not be what it was yesterday, we might lose loved ones (they are aging too), and our days are numbered.

We humans often feel entitled. We assume we'll continue to see the light, eat food, have shelter, and listen to our favorite songs for the rest of our lives. We fail to appreciate what we already have. We could lose everything the very next day. Understand that most people don't wake up in the morning. It's a luxury to see the sun rise again. Just how lucky do you need to be? Death is always hovering above us. We might meet it at the corner of our street, in an accident or from physical illness, or even by falling in the bathroom.

Realize that you are living on borrowed time. You never know when your time will run out. As long as you're here, it's your responsibility to make the most of it. As Oliver Burkeman, author of Four Thousand Weeks and The Antidote, says, we are, on average, going to live just four thousand weeks on this planet. The entirety of your life amounts to roughly 4000 weeks. Depending on your age, you've already lived at least a quarter of it. (As I'm writing this, I'm 25 years old, which means I've lived 1,328 weeks. That leaves 2,672 weeks for me.) Your childhood, school, college, marriage, and work all fit within these weeks. And also, the good deeds you do, what you contribute to the world, and the legacy you leave behind. Those weeks will slip away if we keep thinking we have all the time in the world.

When you remind yourself that you will die one day, you not only come to appreciate life and its beauty but act immediately as well. **Death brings a sense of urgency.** Instead of postponing things to the future (which can't be guaranteed), you'll try to accomplish tasks sooner. You'll get things done. You'll express yourself fully. In doing so, you'll come to understand that you are mortal.

On August 17th, 2018, successful author Robert Greene, known for 48 Laws of Power and Mastery, was going about his day when his girlfriend noticed something was wrong with his face. She immediately pulled the car over and called 911. He passed out and fell into a coma. After being hospitalized, it was revealed that he had suffered a cardiac arrest. Fortunately, he survived. His near-death experience completely transformed him. It made him realize how suddenly death can appear. After his recovery, he began cherishing the little moments with a deep sense of gratitude.

We don't need to have such experiences to appreciate and respect life. However, we can practice Memento Mori and bring ourselves back to reality. Through this practice, we can live a richer and more meaningful life.

The Law of Impermanence

Bhutan is the happiest country in South Asia, not because the government prioritizes its citizens' happiness through Gross National Happiness, but because of the philosophy they follow. One of the key philosophical principles they meditate on is Anitya. Anitya, a Sanskrit word, means the absence of permanence and continuity. If we truly understand this concept and put it into practice, we suffer less and learn to appreciate what we have.

We humans have a tendency to form attachments. We hold on to things for their sentimental value, and there's nothing wrong with that. But pain arises when we lose what we hold dear—specifically, things we are attached to. We fail to appreciate and show gratitude for them when we have them because we feel entitled. We believe we earned and own them. The hard truth, however, is that we don't actually own anything in life.

You might think, "I bought this or that; it's mine." Sure, it is, but here's the point: your life is short, and when you leave your physical body, all your possessions lose their significance. You can't take them with you. They may be passed down to your family, but the things you think you own are nothing but an illusion. If you accept this reality, you'll find peace. You won't be constantly chasing after more possessions.

Attachments cause suffering. We often identify with what we have rather than who we are as individuals. But the moment we accept that everything we own can be taken away by fate, we feel free. We feel liberated. We begin to see things as tools that enhance our lives, not as the essence of our lives. We will appreciate them more; we'll give them our full attention; we'll be more mindful in how we use them. Most importantly, we'll cherish them while they're with us. And when it's time to let go, we'll do so with less pain and suffering.

We should also remind ourselves that change is constant. We can't battle reality. We gain things; we lose things. If you're fixated on what you've lost, you won't be able to embrace the future. But if you accept the impermanence of everything, you'll be able to love what you have and ease your suffering. Life is short—so appreciate the things you possess.

The Law of Ephemerality

At the start of the 20th century, powerful nations sought to establish a presence on the Antarctic continent. This ambition sparked the interest of Ernest Shackleton, an Irish explorer who had already set foot in Antarctica twice before. Shackleton wanted to accomplish something unprecedented: to cross the continent on foot. By then, explorers had reached the South Pole and celebrated their achievements, but no one had traveled the continent from one end to the other. If Shackleton succeeded, it would be a historic feat. With the ship Endurance and a crew of 27, he embarked on the expedition. It wasn't long before Shackleton and his crew realized the hardships awaiting them.

The Endurance became trapped in the Weddell Sea. For the ice to melt and path to clear it will take ten months. However, the ice's pressure eventually crushed their ship, and it sank into the sea. They were now miles from civilization, with dwindling food supplies. To make matters worse, temperatures fell below zero, gusty winds battered them, and the ice they camped on could break at any moment. Waiting for rescue was not an option.

Shackleton knew that survival meant reaching land. With only three lifeboats, they began their journey, with Shackleton leading. Wherever they encountered open water, they boarded the lifeboats and crossed. Eventually, they arrived at Elephant Island. They caught seals and penguins to eat and keep warm, but their ordeal was far from over. Rescue could take years. Shackleton recalled a whaling station he had once visited. If he could reach it, he might convince the station crew to save his men from starvation and death. Yet, it lay 800 miles away. Determined, he set out with five of his strongest men and a large lifeboat, heading into the treacherous sea.

After sailing for 16 days in rough seas, with waves nearly capsizing their lifeboat, Shackleton and his men finally reached the South Georgia whaling station—only to find they had landed on the wrong side. To get help, they needed to hike an additional 36 hours over dangerous terrain. By then, everyone was utterly exhausted, nearly beyond the strength to go on. But Shackleton was determined. Leaving two men with the boat, he and two other crew members set off, climbing 20-foot glaciers and crossing an icy waterfall. Fortunately, people were at the station when they arrived After 5 and a half months Shackleton reached South Georgia Island, all crew members and those left on the other side were saved.

The story of the Imperial Trans-Antarctic Expedition proves that if we endure hardship and face challenges with resilience, we can survive even the harshest of trials. Difficulties grip us in the moment, and our emotions often exaggerate the gravity of our situations, pushing us toward rash reactions that can have serious consequences. Shackleton's calm and steady approach was critical; if he had reacted like anyone else in his crew, they might not have survived. He understood that emotions are contagious and resisted the urge to despair. Rather than cursing his fate, he focused on the next steps and carefully considered his decisions. His resolve and clear thinking ultimately saved his team—and proved him right in the end.

When we face hardships, we often become emotionally overwhelmed, which clouds our thinking and makes it difficult to see a way forward. But if we allow our emotions to subside, solutions start to become clearer. Instead of giving up or avoiding responsibility, we should stand firm and trust in our ability to overcome challenges. Often, **the solution appears if we are patient.**

The law of ephemerality reminds us that everything exists only for a brief time. Situations shift, and emotions pass. When we surrender to fleeting emotions and make impulsive decisions, we risk going dangerously off course. But if we remain patient and wait for clarity, we gain the freedom to choose wisely and respond effectively. Life becomes easier when we respond with patience and perspective.

6

Think Negatively, with a Purpose

"The cave you fear to enter holds the treasure you seek" – Joseph Campbell, author of *A Hero with Thousand Faces.*

Self-help gurus and life coaches have popularized the idea of positive visualization. As the term suggests, it involves imagining all the positive things you want to achieve. Typically, you write these down in a journal and revisit them daily, with the belief that by visualizing your goals, you'll eventually reach them. But this approach can create a disconnect between your mind and reality.

When you focus solely on positive visualization, you may assume that life is linear and predictable—as though hard work and effort will guarantee success. In reality, life is random, and challenges arise unexpectedly. Positive visualization doesn't prepare us for unforeseen obstacles, leaving us vulnerable when we're caught off guard by life's surprises.

As the saying goes, "prevention is better than cure." Preparing for sudden, unexpected situations is more effective than facing them unprepared. Preparation reduces emotional vulnerability, allowing us to remain composed and take measured steps forward. Although it may sound counterintuitive, practicing negative visualization— imagining worst-case scenarios—can help us brace for difficulties.

Negative visualization doesn't mean dwelling on potential misfortunes. Instead, it's about minimizing emotional reactions when hardships arise. By mentally experiencing a challenging situation and the emotions it might evoke, you'll gain insight into how to respond calmly and thoughtfully. When real-life setbacks occur, you're less likely to act impulsively and more likely to stay grounded.

The key to effective negative visualization is maintaining emotional distance. It's easy to get swept away by emotions like anger, which are meant to protect us but can lead to unnecessary worry if left unchecked. As emotions surface during visualization, observe your thoughts and feelings objectively. This self-awareness can offer valuable insights into your personality. When used properly, negative visualization can be a powerful tool in your personal development arsenal.

What's the Worst Thing that Can Happen Today?

After waking up each morning, ask yourself a simple question and meditate on it for a moment. Reflect on your daily routine: the work you do, the commute you take, the people you meet, and the food you eat. Consider where things could go wrong along the way. Perhaps your car might break down, your boss might criticize you, a project might face delays, or your meal might spoil. When these disruptions happen, they can derail your momentum, causing stress and frustration. Lost in emotions and thoughts, you risk wasting valuable time and energy, making it harder to regain your rhythm.

However, if you anticipate such setbacks, you'll maintain your composure and balance, ready to respond. If your car breaks down, you'll have a mechanic's number handy. If work is delayed, you'll identify and avoid distractions that lead to procrastination. In short, you'll have a backup plan. This preparation prevents the situation from robbing you of mental clarity and presence of mind.

Relationships

As we discussed in Chapter 3, relationships can be both a source of profound joy and considerable pain. Human connections—whether with family, friends, or acquaintances—bring color and purpose to life. Sharing moments of success and joy feels incomplete without people around us. Yet, not everyone has our best interests at heart. Many harbor hidden motives, and often, these intentions are not apparent on a first encounter. One can become entangled in the manipulations of others by being overly trusting or naive.

The people we choose to associate with significantly shape our lives. We, as humans, crave validation, appreciation, and attention, which makes us naturally drawn to those who seem to offer it. Yet, people come in many "flavors." On the surface, some may appear kind and generous, but after some time, their true nature emerges, and we may feel disappointment, frustration, or even heartbreak.

Recognizing that not everyone we meet has our well-being in mind can help us manage expectations and avoid unnecessary stress. In most cases, our disappointments stem from our interactions with people—colleagues, classmates, friends, and even family. It's essential to accept that not everyone will act or speak the way we might wish. Many people lack sensitivity or make hurtful remarks unintentionally. If we take their words too seriously, we risk emotional turmoil. (or make hurtful out of bitterness.)

As Marcus Aurelius wrote in Meditations, "When you wake up in the morning, tell yourself: the people I deal with today will be meddling, ungrateful, arrogant, dishonest, jealous, and surly. They are like this because they cannot tell good from evil." Accept people as they are, without expecting them to be just like you. By anticipating flaws and shortcomings, even in those closest to us, we can reduce the pain of disappointment.

Work

Losing a job is one of life's most challenging experiences, and in today's post-COVID-19 job market, it has become a common reality. Hiring has slowed, layoffs are frequent, and as companies increasingly integrate AI, more positions face potential elimination. However, some roles remain relatively "fire-proof," especially those where human creativity and critical analytical skills are irreplaceable. This doesn't mean job security is guaranteed—taking any role for granted could lead to being replaced.

To remain competitive and relevant in your job, consider conducting a monthly self-assessment. Reflect on these key questions:

What new skills should I learn to stay relevant?

What are the recent developments in my field?

How can I apply the feedback I've received?

Where can I improve in my current role?

What are my blind spots?

In today's highly competitive market, securing a job can feel as elusive as finding hidden treasure. For a single position, thousands of applications are often submitted. Many candidates never even receive a response, while only a few get interview calls. Among those, just one person ultimately lands the role. Going through multiple rounds only to face rejection can be disheartening.

Despite these odds, there are ways to improve our chances of getting hired. Regularly refining skills, staying updated, and being proactive in personal development can make all the difference.

Ask yourself these questions:

Why do they have to hire you?

What skills are you bringing to the table?

Why do you think you are the best candidate for the job?

Can you fit into the company's culture?

There are times when you may feel discouraged, but asking yourself questions like these helps keep you grounded and allows you to see things from an employer's perspective. A deadly combination that can hold anyone back is complacency mixed with entitlement—traits that repel both opportunities and people. By confronting reality and adjusting accordingly, you can work toward becoming the ideal candidate employers seek.

Sometimes, even well-qualified individuals don't get the job for reasons that aren't immediately clear. Instead of being discouraged, view it as preparation for the next opportunity. As the Stoic philosopher Seneca wisely put it, "Luck is what happens when preparation meets opportunity." So, create your own luck by staying prepared.

For solopreneurs and freelancers, similar questions apply:

Why should a client choose your service?

What specific value does your service offer?

Have you learned from previous client feedback and improved your offerings?

Are you clearly communicating your services?

Are you consistently delivering the quality you promise?

What new skills or knowledge would allow you to offer premium services?

Regularly reviewing these questions can help you stay competitive, adaptable, and ready to seize the next opportunity that comes your way.

Health

Health is something we often take for granted. We stuff our mouths with all sorts of unhealthy foods—junk, ultra-processed items, fast food, and deep-fried chips. We rarely include vegetables in our meals. This should be the opposite. Yet, despite all the harm we inflict on our bodies, we expect them to function like those of teenagers. **We are what we feed our bodies.** If the input is good, the output is good. That's a basic rule.

As we age, we should recognize that our bodies slowly decay. Our muscles lose mass. Our breathing patterns change. Our bones weaken. Our brains remember less. And if we fall ill, it becomes incredibly difficult to heal and return to a healthy state. The truth is that many of us are aware of these facts, yet we still make no changes to our lifestyle. We then pay the price for our negligence.

We are not like our ancestors. They engaged in intense physical labor almost every day. They had access to organic food, as neighbors would share portions of their harvest in exchange for your grandfather's farm products. They burned enough calories. But we, for the most part, live sedentary lives where the only physical activity we get is 10- to 20-minute walks each day.

We don't limit intake accordingly. We eat, eat, and eat till our tummies look like spare tires.

More than ever, it's essential to take our health seriously. A healthy body enhances productivity, focus, and mental well-being. However, we cannot transform our diets overnight. We need to identify the toxic foods we're consuming and gradually replace them with healthier alternatives. Eating fast food occasionally is fine, but it shouldn't be the go-to choice for daily meals.

Ask yourself these questions and visualize your future health:

If you continue to eat as you do now, will you be fit and active at age 50?

Does the food you eat keep you energized throughout the day?

Are your meals meeting your daily protein and vitamin needs?

What physical activities are you doing to stay fit? Are they enough?

Pro Tip: Make fitness a part of your identity; this will increase your likelihood of sticking to a healthy diet and lifestyle.

Practice Misfortune

Imagine if everything you have—money, property, relationships, everything you've built over the years—was suddenly gone. What would your life look like? It's a frightening thought. We'd never want this to happen, even in our wildest dreams. But whether we admit it or not, we get attached to our accomplishments and possessions. We have a lifestyle that defines us, and we're drawn to life's luxuries. We crave comfort constantly. Instead of viewing possessions as tools to help us reach our goals, we start to see them as extensions of ourselves. Losing them becomes unthinkable.

We are more than the things we own. If we practice misfortune, we can find ease within ourselves, even if ill fate someday leaves us with nothing. Every so often, put on your old clothes. Give up your luxuries—phones, laptops, cars—for a day. Walk barefoot. Eat simple food. Read the classics. The goal is to experience another side of life and recognize how dependent you are on these comforts.

By practicing misfortune, you prepare yourself for real challenges. If adversity strikes, you're more likely to bounce back and start rebuilding. Instead of panicking or feeling defeated, you'll focus on how to reclaim what's lost. This practice lightens the burden, helping you to stand tall and rise above.

Exercise:

Wear your old clothes and go out for a walk with bare feet. Experience humbles you. It proves that no one really cares about you except yourself.

7

What is an Emotion?

"We are born not knowing who we are, we don't know how to think. We only know how to feel. It is through our feelings that how we are raised creates the trajectory for our future lives" – Natasha Khazanov, *a Psychotherapist*

We've spent a great deal of time understanding how the positivity movement can harm mental health, why happiness shouldn't be our ultimate goal, how negative emotions bring depth and meaning to our lives, and why thinking negatively can sometimes limit suffering and pain. But it's essential to understand the roots. Without a foundation, we cannot grasp the bigger picture. **Our appreciation for things depends on how well we understand them.**

It's true that some people experience emotions more intensely than others. To an observer, someone might seem to be overreacting, but that could simply be their natural way of expressing emotions. In some cases, you might feel an emotion strongly, while the person next to you feels nothing—and both reactions are valid. Why? Many factors come into play.

We all grew up in different environments, cultures, and circumstances. Genetics and individual experiences also play crucial roles. All of these elements contribute to what we call the self. Yet, emotions are universal; only the intensity with which we feel them varies from person to person. Recently, research into trauma has begun to explain why some emotions erupt with intensity while others remain dormant. We'll be exploring these topics in more detail soon. For now, we'll delve into the world of emotions: What is an emotion? Why do we, as humans, experience them? And why do negative emotions exist?

Emotion

According to the American Psychological Association (APA), an emotion is "a complex reaction pattern involving experiential, behavioral, and psychological elements." Simply put, a stimulus causes us to feel an emotion. This stimulus can be anything—a color, a painting, music, or the face of a loved one. Often, our emotions are triggered by our thoughts and how we interpret what's happening around us.

Next, there's a physiological response, where the Autonomic Nervous System (ANS) controls our involuntary bodily reactions and determines whether we should fight, flee, or freeze. In a fight response, for instance, the ANS releases a surge of adrenaline into our bloodstream, keeping us alert and ready to defend ourselves. These survival responses have been essential to human evolution and survival.

Finally, there's our behavioral response, which conveys how we feel through facial expressions, body language, and demeanor. Thinking of a loved one might make us feel calm (a physiological response) and smile broadly (a behavioral response). This behavioral response is the outward expression of an emotion, and facial expressions, like emotions, are universal.[1] No matter where we are in the world, a smile looks the same.

But why do we have emotions? In his book How to Know a Person, David Brooks explains, "Emotions contain information. Emotions assign value to things; what we want and what we don't want. Emotions help you adjust to different situations." Emotions exist for a reason; if they were useless, evolution would have discarded them. When we look closely, emotions reveal insights about our inner world, guiding us through circumstances and helping us remember key events. It's a sad but true reality that many of our memories tend to be painful.

Humans are wired with a negative bias—we're naturally more likely to notice and feel negative emotions than positive ones. There's a reason for this. From an evolutionary standpoint, negative emotions help keep us safe. Our ancestors lived in forests, constantly surrounded by threats. When a bush rustled, they couldn't assume it was just the wind; doing so could mean risking their lives. There was always the possibility of a tiger or leopard lurking, waiting for a chance to strike.

Negative emotions heighten our awareness of danger. They make us vigilant about what could go wrong, preparing us for potential threats. Without negative emotions, we likely wouldn't have survived as long as we have. Today, although we live in a much safer world than our ancestors did, our "dangers" are often the people we associate with or collaborate with. Negative emotions still play a role, helping us complete what we start because we want to avoid the losses that could come if we don't stay serious about our efforts.

People who are resilient and have strong emotional regulation often grew up in stable households, where their parents gave them the freedom to develop their own sense of self and shielded them from major traumas, such as physical or emotional abuse. They also benefited from financial security, strong relationships, and access to opportunities. But these are ideal conditions that most of us, myself included, didn't experience. Surviving, in itself, is an accomplishment. Wishing for unattainable things only leads to self-loathing.

The reality is that we all carry trauma. These experiences set the course of our lives. If we're unaware of this impact, it can doom us mentally and emotionally. With awareness, however, we can heal and lessen the hold these experiences have over us.

Trauma

Trauma is the most misused word these days. Failing an exam, not being able to buy the latest iPhone, and losing a valuable thing are not traumatic experiences. Of course, you will be disappointed and mad. But adults are capable of taking disappointments. It will be a momentary feeling; soon we will get back to reality. Trauma runs deep, like an underwater current. **You may not be aware, but trauma affects everything we do—how we feel, how we react, and how we respond to life's disturbing events.**

The word 'trauma' means a wound or an injury. But this wound is not visible. Trauma leaves a wound inside us. As Gabor Mate says in his book The Myth of Normal, "Trauma is not what happens to you; it is what happens inside you as a result of what happens to you." More often than not, wounds remain fresh and painful even though they may appear healed. Experiences similar to those we've been through or triggering words related to a past event can reopen old wounds and make us hurt again. Sadly, we're often unaware of the source and don't understand why we feel the way we do.

Scientifically, psychological trauma is defined as "a person's experience of emotional distress resulting from an event that overwhelms the capacity to emotionally digest it."[2] As adults, we can console ourselves during times of deep pain by talking about it, journaling, or distracting ourselves. But for a child, it's nearly impossible to subdue the agony and distress. In our emotional vulnerability, we begin to develop coping mechanisms that ease the pain but distance us from our authentic selves.

Traumatic experiences actually alter the wiring of our brains. It's well-known that the brain seeks to minimize pain. Once it learns an event is likely to cause pain, it drives us to avoid it. For example, a person who loses loved ones at a young age may grow up avoiding deep connections, fearing the pain of future loss. The loss of a loved one can even make someone wary of loving too deeply again.

People who exhibit overly pleasing behavior may have grown up in environments where parents or guardians didn't meet their emotional needs. As we've discussed, humans crave attention, appreciation, approval, and love. Those who missed out on these things in childhood often keep searching for them. They think that by being nice, suppressing their own needs, and doing everything others want, they'll finally receive the love they crave. But in the process, they often end up disappointed and hurt when others don't reciprocate. **Love isn't something we should have to search for; it's something we should be able to receive.**

When parents are absent, children are often forced to become self-reliant at an early age. They feel they shouldn't be a burden to their families and strive to meet expectations, cultivating an image of independence. On the surface, they may appear to have carried themselves well throughout life, but the reality is often different. Internally, they struggle with mental difficulties. Though they may seem happy, they carry an emotional void, feeling incomplete despite having what they need. They often grapple with self-doubt and face challenges in forming close relationships—outcomes of an emotionally deprived childhood.

Unfortunately, some of us endured sexual or emotional abuse as children. At a young age, it's difficult to discern what's normal versus harmful. By the time we reach an age where we understand the nature of these experiences, trauma has already taken root within us. Repeated sexual assault, in particular, can have lasting impacts, making it challenging for survivors to recover fully. They may become hypersensitive to perceived threats, constantly recalling and reliving their past trauma.

When such abuse is compounded by other traumatic experiences—emotional neglect, loss of loved ones, witnessing or experiencing domestic violence—the likelihood of developing mental and physical health issues in adulthood increases. This long-term trauma can manifest as extreme anxiety, anger, sadness, or even an inability to feel pleasure, affecting various facets of life.[3]

If your father was an alcoholic who often came home creating turmoil, you might have developed hyper-vigilance, constantly scanning your environment for potential threats. Growing up feeling unsafe and trapped can lead to heightened alertness, where even a sudden sound triggers an instinctive need to identify its source. Despite being in a safe environment, these experiences can activate your brain's survival circuits, making it hard to relax. **For children who witness domestic violence, this constant vigilance often affects concentration and can hinder academic performance.**

Trauma can also be the root of persistent negative thoughts. When faced with setbacks, you might start believing it's your fault, questioning if you're inadequate or fearing others' judgments. These self-blaming patterns can snowball from minor inconveniences, building into a cascade of negative thoughts. Often, this is your inner child speaking—the vulnerable part of you that once felt powerless. **Part of healing involves "parenting" yourself, offering reassurance and support to soothe that inner child.**

Because we're often unaware of how trauma influences our thoughts, many of us instinctively try to replace negative thoughts with positive ones. When that doesn't work, we attempt to suppress them. However, two things happen here: first, suppressed thoughts tend to resurface, often more powerfully. Second, without understanding the root cause, genuine healing remains elusive. Healing begins with awareness. Though suppressing emotions might feel like a temporary solution, unaddressed feelings can create deeper emotional turmoil over time.

If we're not suppressing our emotions, we often end up ruminating—caught in a loop of repetitive thoughts with no resolution. Surprisingly, some people become attached to their thoughts, finding even negative ones familiar and oddly comforting because they've spent so much time with them. Venturing beyond this familiar mental space can feel unsettling, and they may resist seeing other perspectives. However, rumination is mentally exhausting, leaving little room for joy or enthusiasm for life. Often, it isn't their fault; early life experiences may have led them to feel unworthy or inadequate. Yet, **rumination without resolution becomes a path to self-destruction.**

Trauma affects everyone, and it can either strengthen or weaken us. It's important not to let past experiences define who we are today. As Edith Eger writes in The Choice, instead of asking, "Why me?" it's more empowering to ask, "What now?" Rather than focusing on why something happened, shifting our attention to what we can do next is essential for moving forward. **Healing involves making peace with the past, releasing what holds us back, allowing ourselves to feel emotions we've been suppressing, and expressing what has remained unsaid.**

In the next chapter, we'll explore how to fully experience emotions and build emotional regulation using proven techniques.

8

A Guide to Emotional Self-Regulation

**"Understanding is the first step to acceptance,
and only with acceptance can there be recovery"
– J.K Rowling, author of *Harry Potter and The
Goblet of Fire***

We were never taught how to feel emotions. Instead, we have been instructed by our parents, teachers, and authority figures to suppress certain emotions when we experience them. The problem with society is that it categorizes some emotions as more desirable than others. We are expected to feel and express only the emotions that others approve of, while negative emotions are to be kept to ourselves. We have been taught how to cultivate positive emotions, yet the others are ignored. This is the process of abandoning our true selves.

We all collectively agree that intense negative emotions can be damaging—they can ruin families, careers, and lives. Anger, for example, is a devastating force if it is not kept within limits and channeled productively. When you are angry, you are told to suppress the emotion, but this only makes it more dangerous. The more you suppress an emotion, the more powerful it becomes. Once it explodes, it can leave you with devastating consequences.

Our goal should be to understand what our emotions are trying to convey. As discussed in the previous chapter, emotions help us adapt to the situations we face. It is important to pay attention to what they are saying. In other words, we must process our emotions, fully embrace them, and gradually release them from our bodies. Sadly, we were never taught this, and now we are facing the consequences.

Studies have shown that "failing to process emotions causes anxiety, depression, and stress." People who cannot process emotions often resort to harmful coping mechanisms, such as "avoidance, self-harm, emotional eating, rumination, escapism, aggression, and substance abuse." [1] Carl Jung, the renowned psychotherapist, put it this way: "People will do anything, no matter how absurd, to avoid facing their own soul"—because they haven't learned how to.

Conversely, people who can process their emotions are better decision-makers and navigate tough situations more effectively. When a situation evokes strong emotions, they know how to calm themselves and consider the best course of action. Of course, emotions often take center stage and overwhelm us, but after a while, we return to our default state. We are not perfect, and we don't have to be. **To be human is to be incomplete.** However, we shouldn't let our momentary emotional reactions determine the course we wish to avoid. Our goal should be to keep learning how to process emotions with ease.

What Exactly Are You Feeling?

Human beings are good at noticing emotions in others but not in themselves. We can read facial expressions and discern what a person is going through. We can observe body gestures, movements, and posture and conclude that a person might need help or that we should maintain distance. We are programmed this way, a gift shaped by years of evolution. But the fact remains: we struggle to introspect ourselves.

The first step is identifying what emotion or feeling you are experiencing. It sounds easy, but human emotions are complex, and we often mistake one for another. A wrong diagnosis leads to the wrong treatment, and the wrong treatment doesn't yield the results we want. With the wide spectrum of feelings we experience, it can seem like a daunting task to pinpoint what we are feeling and work through it. It is difficult, but not impossible. All it takes is an awareness of the emotional vocabulary and an understanding of the situations that typically evoke those emotions.

We all know six basic emotions—Sadness, Happiness, Fear, Anger, Disgust, and Surprise. However, according to a recent study, we only have four primary emotions—Happiness, Sadness, Fear/Surprise, and Anger/Disgust. Yet, we don't feel the same emotion in every situation. Our emotions shift according to our circumstances. Because we are familiar with only these four major emotions, we often assign one of them to the feeling we are currently experiencing, even though emotions encompass a range of feelings. Using broad terms can prevent us from truly understanding what we are feeling.

When people say they are sad, they might actually be feeling lonely, despair, hurt, depressed, or even guilty. Instead of digging deeper, they often retreat to simply labeling it as sadness. To truly understand ourselves and get closer to our emotional states, we need to pinpoint exactly what we are experiencing. Only through accurate identification can we know how we truly feel. Fortunately, Dr. Gloria Willcox developed a feeling wheel that untangles the complexity of emotions, helping individuals identify and articulate their emotions more precisely.

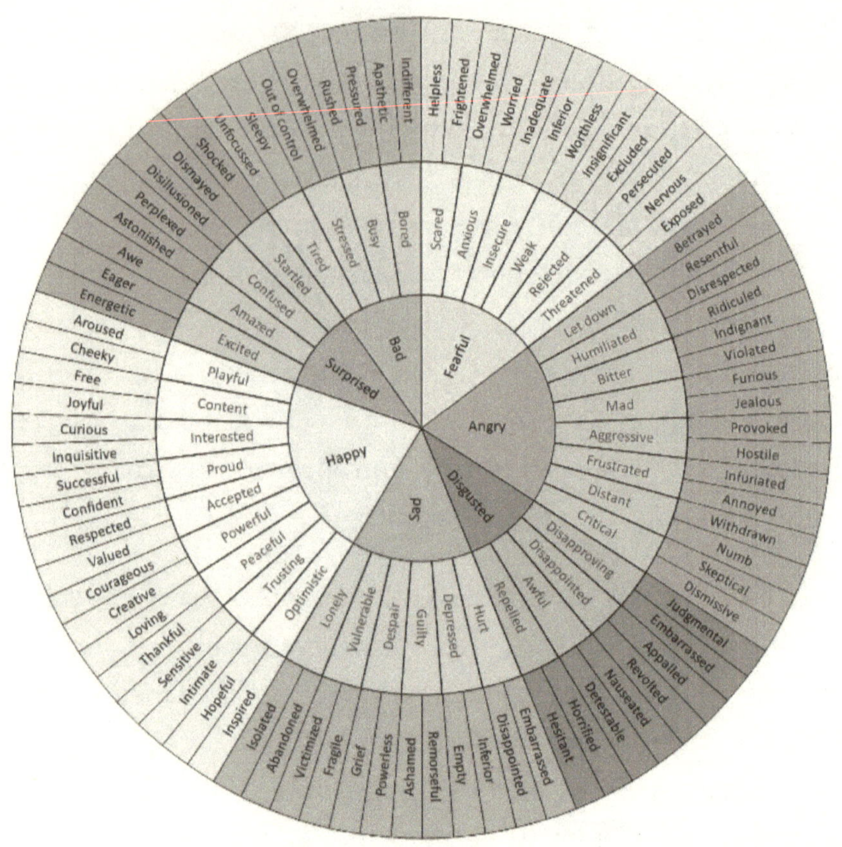

Source: https://feelingswheel.com/

When you are undergoing an emotion, dig through the wheel and find out the feelings are in categories and subcategories. Do it regularly, you will have a better awareness of your emotional dispositions.

Sit With Your Feelings

Now comes the hardest part of the process. Unpleasant emotions or feelings stir up our minds, becoming so unbearable that we want to do anything and everything except face them. Our human nature is to avoid what makes us uncomfortable. But we must build the courage to nudge ourselves into sitting with these emotions.

Once you've identified the feeling or emotion, find a quiet space free from distractions—no phone, laptop, or TV.

Ask yourself the following questions and write your answers in your journal:

What thoughts is this emotion stirring in me?

Are these thoughts negative or positive?

If they are negative, what are they trying to convey?

How are these thoughts affecting my mood right now?

How am I reacting?

Where exactly am I feeling this emotion in my body?

Can I notice any bodily reactions?

Is this the first time I've felt this way?

If it isn't, when did I last feel this way?

Did something or someone trigger this emotion?

If so, what exactly is triggering me?

What can I do to avoid getting triggered the next time?

What is this emotion trying to tell me?

As you do this exercise, remember that it's important not to let your thoughts carry you away. Instead, observe the thoughts and the feelings they evoke. Set a timer for 20 minutes, and during that time, allow yourself to fully feel the emotion. When the timer goes off, return to reality.

You can also express the emotion through your body. If it's anger, for example, shout it out into empty space. The key here is to release the emotion—whether through expression or simply acknowledging it. As Edith Eger says, "Expression is the opposite of depression." Don't keep your feelings or emotions inside. Express them.

Radical Acceptance

When we are emotionally overwhelmed, we tend to blame ourselves for things that are beyond our control. We ask ourselves, "Why is this happening to me?" "Why me?" Although external factors affect us emotionally, externalizing our emotions doesn't help calm us down. Instead, we might make a hurtful remark or say something mean to get satisfaction from the pain others have caused us. Some may even go as far as seeking revenge. As Edith Eger wisely says about revenge: "Revenge is not evolving; it is revolving around the same thing over and over again." We should avoid doing that.

This is not to say you should let people say or do hurtful things to you. You must set boundaries and communicate them clearly. However, the more important thing here is accepting your emotions. You need to acknowledge what you're feeling and accept your emotions as they arise—by verbalizing them.

When you feel anger, say it out loud to yourself: "I am feeling angry." Express just how angry you are: "I feel like punching the guy." **Verbalizing your feelings or emotions helps neutralize them. You're taking the intensity out of the emotion, making it less likely that you'll act impulsively.** Once a word or deed is said or done, it cannot be undone. So, accept your feelings and emotions. Do it wholeheartedly. Completely.

Journaling

You've probably heard about it a lot. I agree, it's oversaturated in everyone's mind, but it works for most people. It helps me understand what I'm feeling.

Writing untangles the messy knots of our thoughts. It helps declutter our minds, as thoughts tend to be random. One thought leads to another, and before we know it, we're overthinking—nothing good comes from it. Instead, overthinking drains our energy and leads to procrastination on important tasks. By writing down random thoughts on paper, we make them predictable. We trace back to the source: Why am I feeling this way? Journaling provides clarity. It helps clear our headspace and improve our mood. It's no secret that many people feel better after writing down their concerns.

Freek Van Litsenburb, on his Instagram account @wethinkdeeply, shared three compelling and thought-provoking questions that can help reset your life:

What activity makes you lose track of time completely?

Which object, person, or experience brought you the most joy as a child?

If you lived the last seven days forever, where would it lead you? Would it take you to a life well-lived or a coffin full of regrets?[2]

How to be Present

Spiritual gurus often talk about living in the moment, but they don't tell us how to achieve it. They vaguely suggest shutting down our thoughts and focusing on the task at hand. However, the stresses of everyday life catch up with us. There are so many things demanding our time and energy, yet we struggle to allocate them effectively. Our energy is limited. We can only focus for 4-6 hours a day; beyond that, our minds start to wander. To truly live in the moment, we need to increase our tolerance levels.

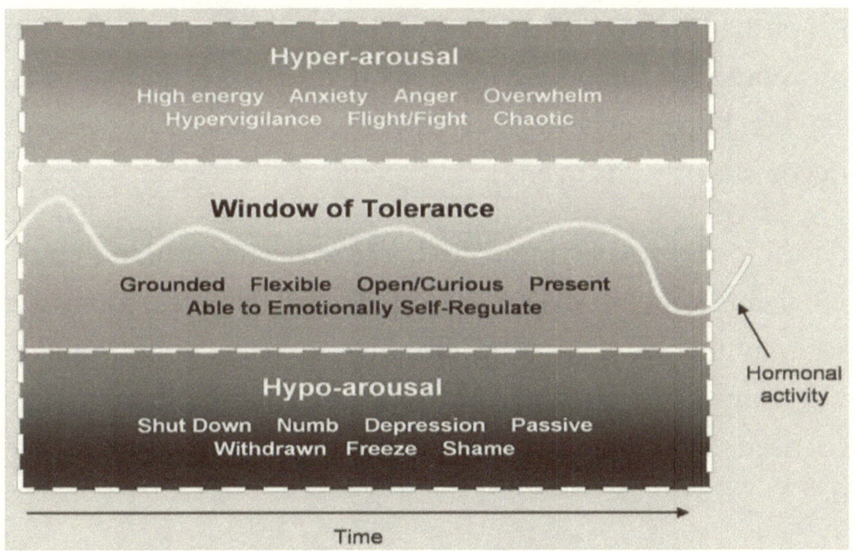

Source:https://www.gov.je/SiteCollectionDocuments/Education/ID%2
0The%20Window%20of%20Tolerance%2020%2006%2016.pdf

Dan Siegel, a renowned psychiatrist, developed the concept of the Window of Tolerance. Simply put, the Window of Tolerance refers to your personal capacity to tolerate stress and handle complex emotions and challenging experiences.[3] When we are within this window, we are in an ideal state of mind. We can face challenges and stress more effectively, without internal resistance. We are grounded, curious, and—more importantly—present. Difficult tasks do not derail our focus or presence of mind.

At the top of the window lies Hyperarousal. In this state, we feel threatened by the slightest inconvenience. We feel anxious, constantly scanning our surroundings for potential threats, and may feel an urge to escape the moment. We become hypersensitive to lights and sounds, staying hypervigilant. Our tolerance is low, and we can become easily annoyed.

At the bottom is Hypoarousal, a less discussed state. Here, we feel numb and disconnected. There are moments when we may feel like giving up entirely—exhausted and unable to engage in any activity. At other times, we become hyper-focused on details, striving for perfection in everything we do.

Naturally, we often oscillate between these two states, as life can be overwhelming. However, it doesn't have to be this way. We can be present. While it is easier said than done, we can challenge ourselves, little by little. By observing our responses to stress, we can identify healthy and effective coping mechanisms. Journaling our thoughts, improving our sleep patterns, exercising regularly, and spending time in nature are all practices that can help. With increased tolerance, we can manage stress and stay focused in the present moment.

Mindfulness

We often operate in autopilot mode. More often than not, we become so absorbed by our thoughts that we forget our surroundings, where we are, and what we are doing. Mindless thinking steals our ability to truly interact with people and our environment.

Dr. Julie Smith, in her book Why Has Nobody Told Me This Before?, explains that mindfulness "means paying attention to the present moment, with awareness of thoughts, feelings, and bodily sensations that arise, without judgment or distraction." **To be mindful means to observe your thoughts without giving them power.** Even when they are unpleasant or disturbing, simply observe. Once you give them power, an army of unwanted thoughts will flood your mind, and you'll find yourself overthinking.

Practice R.A.I.N

This mindfulness exercise was introduced by Michelle McDonald and later developed by Tara Brach.

R – Recognition: Ask yourself, "What am I feeling right now?"

A – Allow: Allow the emotion to fully take over. Don't try to avoid or suppress it. Simply observe the sensations in your body.

I – Investigate: What emotions are you experiencing? Why do you feel this way? Be curious.

N – Nurture: Be kind to yourself. Don't criticize yourself for your feelings and emotions. Be grateful for what you have and take a moment to remember your loved ones.

Emotional Competence

Emotional competence involves not suppressing emotions but instead expressing them within healthy emotional boundaries. Dr. Gabor Maté, a renowned physician, emphasizes the importance of emotional competence. In his book When the Body Says No, he explains that it "protects us from the hidden stresses that pose a risk to our health, and it is essential to regain if we are to heal."

To be emotionally competent, Dr. Maté asserts, we must have the ability to feel our emotions and express them effectively. We must also set boundaries with others and be mindful of our needs that require fulfillment. He strongly believes that trying to be emotionless is dangerous and can lead to illness. Feel your emotions, and express them.

How to Choose a Right Therapist

We can't do everything on our own. Often, we need external help to understand what we're going through. While friends and family are often ready to support us and be a part of our healing process, they have their limitations. They don't always know exactly what's going on in our minds. It's often best to seek professional help, where we not only feel heard and understood, but also receive advice on how to better cope with our emotions.

It's important to note that a therapist cannot magically fix your problems. Therapy is a space where we open up fully and discover ourselves from a new perspective. Often, the solutions to our struggles are already right in front of us. A few thoughtful questions from the therapist can help us realize what we've been missing and how to move toward healing. This brings us to the question: how do we choose the right therapist?

Opening up about our vulnerabilities takes courage. If we find ourselves with a bad therapist, it can leave us feeling misunderstood and cheated. Even if we find the right therapist later, previous negative experiences can make it harder to open up. It's crucial to find a good therapist who is experienced in the area you need help with and shows empathy. Some therapists are impatient and rush to diagnose without first understanding the client's emotional state. These are the ones we need to avoid.

The first step is to identify what problems you are facing. Based on this, you can determine whether to see a psychologist or psychiatrist. If you're dealing with stress, anxiety, or relationship issues, a psychologist may be a good fit. If you're experiencing depressive episodes, suicidal thoughts, or chronic anxiety, a psychiatrist might be necessary, as they can prescribe medication if needed. You can ask your family doctor or another healthcare professional for a referral. Then, book an appointment—whether in-person or via a virtual meeting.

After the initial meeting, ask yourself the following questions:

Am I comfortable opening up?

Did I feel that the therapist was truly listening to me?

Did the therapist rush the session or attempt to diagnose without understanding my emotional state?

And most importantly, is this therapist affordable?

If you feel unsure after the first meeting, it may be worth finding someone else. Remember, finding the right therapist is crucial for your healing. You need someone who makes you feel safe and comfortable sharing your feelings and thoughts. Therapy is not a taboo—it's a space for untangling your emotions and discovering yourself in a new light.

$$9$$

What Rituals Teach Us

"Ritual is able to hold the long-discarded shards of our stories and make them whole again. It has the strength and elasticity to contain what we cannot contain on our own, what we cannot face in solitude" - Francis Weller, *a Psychotherapist.*

As humans, we follow traditions and rituals for a reason. Behind each ritual lies a deeply embedded philosophy. In modern times, however, we often perform these rituals blindly, without understanding their significance. The true purpose of a ritual is to remind us of the philosophy and wisdom it embodies. Without this understanding, rituals become little more than ordinary human activities.

I'd like to introduce you to a tradition we follow in our state in India. It carries a rich philosophy that encourages us to embrace all aspects of life and appreciate their presence.

Ugadi Pachadi

I'm from the southern state of Telangana in India, where we celebrate the Telugu New Year, Ugadi, usually in March or April. On this auspicious day, we prepare Ugadi Pachadi, a soup with a diverse range of tastes. It's simple to make and can be enjoyed right away. The ingredients you'll need are jaggery powder, neem flowers, an unripened green mango, tamarind, pepper, and salt. Mix them all in the right proportions, and it's ready. You can drink it or eat it with a spoon. But don't be fooled by the individual taste of each ingredient. When combined, it's utterly delicious.

Here's the key: all six ingredients represent six human emotions. Jaggery (sweet) symbolizes happiness, neem flowers (bitterness) symbolize surprises, unripened green mango symbolizes sadness, tamarind (sour) symbolizes unpleasantness, salt (salty) symbolizes the uncertainty of life, and pepper (spicy) symbolizes anger. Human life is a blend of all these emotions.

If one ingredient overpowers the others, the taste won't be balanced. Similarly, we shouldn't wish for happiness alone. True happiness comes from experiencing a range of emotions. Life is well-lived and appreciated when we embrace all kinds of experiences, both positive and negative. **Ugadi Pachadi carries an important message: a mix of all emotions makes life beautiful.**

Part 3

"To be yourself in a world that is constantly trying to make you something else is the greatest accomplishment"
– Ralph Waldo Emerson, an American Philosopher

10

Unconventional but Life-Changing Advice

**"Normal is not something to aspire to,
it's something to get away from"
Jodie Foster, *An Actress and Filmmaker***

Society expects you to act and function in ways that serve its own interests. You get overwhelmed by worldly expectations and responsibilities that are often impossible to fulfill. As a result, you experience burnout and suffering. To reduce your pain and feel more alive, you need to reject toxicity disguised as 'normal.' The following concepts will help you reconnect with your true self, enrich your life, ease the burden of being human, and allow you to be authentic.

Learn to say No

We often pile up our commitments, accepting more and more work just to avoid appearing selfish. We take on others' tasks, leading to physical and mental exhaustion. We attend gatherings because we fear what people will think if we don't. We say yes to things even when our schedule is already full. In all these situations, we prioritize others and neglect ourselves. What matters is how we feel, not what others think of us. If you feel like going, go and have fun. If you don't, kindly explain why you can't. People will understand. **Always remember, the more readily available you are to others, the less you value yourself.** Learn to say no to things you don't want to do.

Set Boundaries

Boundaries reflect how much we respect ourselves. The absence of boundaries exposes our people-pleasing behavior and the cost of neglecting our own needs. More often than not, people say hurtful and mean things. If you don't stand up for yourself and express how their words make you feel, they will likely repeat the behavior, and you'll continue feeling bad. It's understandable to fear how others might react when you share your feelings, but your self-worth should come first. No one else will do that for you. Set boundaries with others. Let them know when they are crossing your limits and testing your tolerance. Always stay true to your feelings. Listen to them, and act accordingly.

Cut Ties with Toxic people

Toxic people know how to make their presence felt in your life. They belittle you, behaving as if they are superior. They gaslight you, making you believe you are the problem. They are dramatic, and even the slightest remark from you can send them into a rage. They don't listen to your feelings or opinions. Their way is the only way. Life with toxic people is unbearable and tests your will to live. Often, toxic people are the closest to you, and you may feel powerless to do anything about it.

But there is always something you can do: choose yourself first. Prioritize your needs, desires, interests, and your purpose in life. Try sharing your feelings with toxic people and make them understand what you're going through. If they don't listen, distance yourself. If they continue to harass you, cut ties with them. What's the point of maintaining relationships that don't provide peace or a sense of belonging? Relationships should be harmonious and supportive—or at the very least, neutral, not destructive.

Letting go of loved ones is difficult, especially when they've been a part of your life for so long. But you must put that behind you and move forward. **Remember, at any stage of your life, you can form new relationships and live joyfully.** You have a choice: stay stuck in a toxic environment or gather the strength to renew your life. The choice is yours.

Be Minimalist

Most of our desires are manufactured. Society and culture have conditioned us to believe we need bigger, better things. But when we stop to think, we realize we don't need much. To keep up with others, we buy things we don't really want. We feel the need to signal to society that we can afford luxury—showing off the latest iPhone or an expensive car. Unknowingly, we fall into a trap.

Minimalism isn't about getting rid of everything we own; it's about buying only what truly adds value to our lives. A car is a necessity in today's world, but you don't need a BMW— a Toyota will suffice. The key is understanding how our 'wants' enhance our lives. They should lift us up, not weigh us down. Be mindful of your purchases. Ask yourself: How does this product add value to my life?

Be Authentic

Being authentic means embracing who you truly are. We live in a world where society pressures you to conform, stifling your uniqueness and pushing you to follow the crowd. It's time to reclaim your birthright—to express yourself fully. Strengthen your core talents and unlock your potential. It may feel daunting, but it's worth every step. You are not a sheep; you are a human being brimming with creativity and passion.

Immerse yourself in Literature

Reading great works of the past can be humbling. They remind you that there is always more to learn and that others may possess greater wisdom. Classic literature can be challenging to follow: long paragraphs, lengthy dialogues, and at times, unengaging prose. Yet, these works often reflect the depths of human nature and psychology, revealing the complexity of the human soul. They provoke deep moral reflection. If you immerse yourself in them, your perspective on life can shift permanently. Consider reading the works of Fyodor Dostoevsky and Friedrich Nietzsche.

Life is Random, Luck Plays a Major Role

We often believe that life is linear and predictable. We're taught that if we work hard enough, success is guaranteed—it's the mantra of Silicon Valley. Entrepreneurs frequently speak of hard work and sacrifice, but there's another side to the story. By focusing solely on achievements and success stories, we overlook the efforts of those who fall short. The simple truth is that luck favors a few and overlooks the majority. It's not your fault—that's just the way life works. Don't be hard on yourself if you put in tremendous effort and still fail. Sometimes, luck simply isn't on your side.

Don't Follow a Script

Even before we are born, a life script is written for us—a blueprint for how to live. This script exists across all cultures around the world. It dictates what to study, what career to pursue, when to marry, how to have children, how to retire, and even how to die. It's the path of least resistance. Going against the script brings uncertainty, and others may not support us. Doubts creep in: What if I fail? Anxiety takes hold, and instead of choosing the courageous route, we return to the script.

Understand that there is no single way to live life. You can live it your own way. You must have faith in yourself and the courage to fully support your decisions. Even if you fail (though I hope you won't), you can always resort to the infamous script. Don't be afraid of what others might think. At least you tried something that 99% of people won't. Be bold. Be you.

Ask Right Questions

The right questions lead to the right answers. We often find ourselves circling the same issue repeatedly when we lack clarity about where we are and what we're doing. To gain clarity, we must ask the right questions. To uncover the truth from someone, we need to ask calibrated, yet direct questions. To truly understand what a person is going through, the right questions can reveal that. Right answers fill the void of doubt. It takes time, but with practice, you'll get better at asking the right questions.

Silence is Expensive

We usually keep track of things that are becoming more expensive daily: gold, diamonds, rent, groceries, etc. But as more people flock to cities, there's one commodity that's becoming increasingly scarce: silence. Human beings perform at their best in a quiet environment. Creative ideas flourish when there's no noise around. Our productivity peaks when there's no one or nothing to disturb us. Our human interactions are more joyful and meaningful when we can give ourselves fully, without distractions. Silence enhances everything we do.

If you ask anyone if they can stay in a silent environment for an hour without doing anything, most people will become uncomfortable. **We're so used to the constant noise that silence feels unsettling.** It should be the other way around. We need to return to our roots, when humans spent much of their time in quiet reflection. It's harder to find that silence in the city, but that's why we need to make time for 'silent retreats' every week. Find a place to unplug and immerse yourself in silence. Hiking or camping in the woods can be a great way to achieve that. Discover what works best for you, and cultivate it. Silence is essential for mental health, and it's becoming increasingly difficult to afford.

Silliness is Divine

Life flows more smoothly when we don't take everything too seriously. Of course, some aspects of life require seriousness—otherwise, we risk ruining everything we've worked for. But that doesn't mean we should be stern and focused all the time. It's exhausting. Problems are just obstacles in our path, and obsessing over them won't help us move forward. More often than not, problems resolve themselves when we let go and do nothing. To feel truly alive, you need to embrace silliness. Let your heart run free, talk about whatever brings you joy, and share genuine laughs. Being content with who we are brings out our best side.

Be Selectively Nice with People

Some people don't deserve our empathy or consideration. They are opportunists, always looking for ways to take advantage of you. If you're too nice, you'll become their prey. They will latch onto you, draining your emotional energy. By the time you realize what's happening, it might be too late. Before calling someone a friend or allowing them into your close circle, keep a safe distance and observe their behavior. If they praise you excessively or try to make you feel like a hero, these are signs you should keep them at arm's length. Be kind to the people who genuinely appreciate you for who you are, not for what they can gain from you.

Wonder about Everything

Human life is a miracle. To be born and experience the world is an extraordinary gift. As a child, your curiosity knows no bounds. You ask endless questions: Why does this look the way it does? How do things work? What's its purpose? You have an insatiable hunger for knowledge and understanding. As we grow older, however, that trait slowly fades away. We become more rigid in our thinking. Our interests shift, and soon, the most pressing question becomes which celebrity is involved with whom.

The truth is, we only live for about four thousand weeks. In that short time, we barely scratch the surface of the vast body of knowledge available. There is so much to learn that even ten lifetimes wouldn't be enough. But if you maintain your curiosity and sense of wonder, you will find joy in the world around you. Every day will present itself as a new marvel.

You need to rediscover the child within. Set aside time—at least four hours each week—to learn something new about the world. If you read books, you're already on the path to knowledge. Remember, learning should be for its own sake, not merely for utility. Be a lifelong learner.

Above all, strive to be a good human. Be humble. Avoid causing harm. And, always pay attention to your work. By doing so, you'll eliminate much of the stress in your life.

11

Conclusion

I've seen individuals try to solve problems with positivity, often struggling in the process. They want to get things done and make things work, believing that positivity can help them reach their goals, as promised in many self-help books. The issue with this belief is that positivity doesn't address the root cause; it might only treat the symptoms. But real progress comes from working on the source, where the problem begins.

As we discussed in Chapter 2, an obsession with positivity prevents us from introspecting. It stifles growth and clouds our ability to see things as they truly are. It pushes us to suppress our emotions and feelings, creating the illusion that everything will always work out as planned. This illusion can be dangerous. We are already emotionally vulnerable, and when things don't go as we expect, we can explode. This can destroy everything we've worked for.

In moments of uncertainty, telling ourselves a few positive affirmations can help us cope. But unless these affirmations are realistic and grounded in the effort we're putting into achieving something, positivity might only make us feel worse. We become desperate to feel 'positive,' when what we really need is to focus on something meaningful. This provides us with the direction and drive to excel in life. Meaningful work offers satisfaction and fulfillment.

Instead of obsessing over positivity and happiness, we should cultivate meaning in our lives. It's through meaningful work that we can give ourselves fully, form genuine relationships where we can be our true selves, and appreciate the beauty around us. Nature reveals its beauty when we are open to it. Meaning gives us the strength to endure difficulties.

Some things are more valuable than others. Often, the things that challenge us the most enrich our lives. Regrets, mistakes, and negative experiences are inevitable, but they pave the path to growth. If we view them as opportunities to learn and improve, we become wiser. We should wish for what we can learn, rather than hoping to avoid these experiences altogether.

To become whole, we must accept the inevitable. One such reality is death. Meditating on death compels us to act quickly on what truly matters and helps us appreciate life. Our desires often cloud our minds, preventing us from appreciating what we already have. By recognizing the impermanence of things, we can better understand their value and reduce our pain when it's time to let go. In the face of apparent death, we can endure hardship by reminding ourselves that adversities are temporary. Shackleton's incredible story is a testament to this.

Intentionally thinking negatively serves a purpose. It helps us recognize what we are missing, uncover our blind spots, and identify opportunities for success. By considering negative aspects of life—whether in career, health, or relationships—we become aware of where we might make mistakes and can take steps to avoid them.

Emotions carry valuable information. They exist for a reason and reflect our internal state. It is up to us to understand and process them. Trauma can influence the intensity of our emotions. Years of unresolved trauma cannot be erased by positive thinking alone; it must be untangled and healed. To truly understand our emotional states, we must first address the trauma beneath them.

Suppression occurs when we fail to process our emotions. Intense feelings make us emotionally vulnerable, as discussed throughout the book. We often think that distracting ourselves is the only solution, but that is not the case. Unexpressed emotions inevitably resurface and create more difficulty in our lives. Now more than ever, it is crucial to process and regulate our emotions (see Chapter 8).

Rituals are deeply rooted in philosophy. The philosophy behind rituals is why we engage in them in the first place. In modern times, we've forgotten the significance and meaning of many rituals. For example, Ugadi Pachadi teaches us that to live a beautiful and fulfilling life, we must experience the full spectrum of emotions and navigate both the highs and lows of life.

The central message of this book is that we need all kinds of experiences in life. We shouldn't seek only positive experiences, which can distort our view of reality. Likewise, we shouldn't immerse ourselves in negativity, as it drains the joy from life. We need both positive and negative experiences to maintain balance. Look for ways to learn from negative experiences, as they help keep you grounded and realistic.

The ideas in this book reflect my personal beliefs and practices. In many ways, it serves as a manual for living. Whenever I find myself stuck in a rut, I turn to these concepts for guidance and emerge stronger. I hope this book can serve as a manual for you, too.

Acknowledgments

I would like to express my deepest gratitude to my Sweetie for her unwavering support throughout the writing process. She ensured that I stayed on track and maintained the quality of my work. Her understanding of my emotional and physical absence during this time meant the world to me. I am forever grateful for her feedback on the initial drafts, which played a crucial role in shaping the book. Without her, this book wouldn't be what it is today.

I am immensely grateful to my mother, Aruna, who has been my constant support, always there for me. With the utmost pride, I can say that I owe my life to her. No matter how much I give, I will always be in her debt. I wish, if I could live a thousand lives, that she could be my mother in each one.

I want to thank my sister and friends—Pravallika, Jeevan, and Thriveni—for being my pillars of strength. They are always there for me, ensuring that I'm doing okay. I am beyond thankful for their presence in my life.

Even during moments of feeling stuck, I never gave up on writing. It has been my solace, a healing balm for my soul. I want to thank myself for having the courage to believe in and follow my creative calling.

Recommended Reading

Yes to Life: In Spite of Everything by Viktor E. Frankl

When the Body Says No: The Cost of Hidden Stress by Gabor Maté

The Myth of Normal: Trauma, Illness, and Healing in a Toxic Culture by Gabor Maté and Daniel Maté

What Happened to You? Conversations on Trauma, Resilience, and Healing by Bruce D. Perry and Oprah Winfrey

The Child in You: The Breakthrough Method for Bringing Out Your Authentic Self by Stefanie Stahl

Bittersweet: How Sorrow and Longing Make Us Whole by Susan Cain

The Pyramid Mind by Vlad Beliavsky

Thinking in Bets: Making Smarter Decisions When You Don't Have All the Facts by Annie Duke

The Other Side of Happiness: Embracing a More Fearless Approach to Living by Brock Bastian

Quit: The Power of Knowing When to Walk Away by Annie Duke

The Comfort Crisis: Embrace Discomfort to Reclaim Your Wild, Happy, Healthy Self by Michael Easter

The Black Swan: The Impact of the Highly Improbable by Nassim Nicholas Taleb

Fooled by Randomness: The Hidden Role of Chance in Life and in the Markets by Nassim Nicholas Taleb

Man's Search for Meaning by Viktor E. Frankl

Atomic Habits: An Easy & Proven Way to Build Good Habits and Break Bad Ones by James Clear

Why Has Nobody Told Me This Before? by Dr. Julie Smith

The Practice of Groundedness: A Transformative Path to Success That Feeds, Not Crushes, Your Soul by Brad Stulberg

References

Part 1

Chapter 1: Positivity, a Modern-day Scam

Moyer, M. W. (2023, April 21). Lean Into Negative Emotions. It's the Healthy Thing to Do. *The New York Times*. https://www.nytimes.com/2023/04/21/well/mind/negative-emotions-mental-health.html

Toxic Positivity. (n.d.). Taking Charge of Your Survivorship. https://www.takingcharge.csh.umn.edu/survivorship/toxic-positivity

Chapter 2: How Positivity Obsession Ruining Your Life

Stokes, V. (2020, September 8). *Surprising Benefits of Negative Thinking*. Healthline; Healthline Media. https://www.healthline.com/health/positive-side-negative-thinking#takeaway

Rodriguez, T. (2013). Taking the Bad with the Good. *Scientific American Mind*, *24*(2), 26–27. https://doi.org/10.1038/scientificamericanmind0513-26

Brooks, A. C. (2020, June 18). *Sit With Negative Emotions, Don't Push Them Away*. The Atlantic.

https://www.theatlantic.com/family/archive/2020/06/dont-push-away-your-negative-emotions/613180/

Reynolds, G. (2022, September 23). *Toxic Positivity*. Adaa.org. https://adaa.org/learn-from-us/from-the-experts/blog-posts/consumer/toxic-positivity

Lilienfeld, S. O., & Arkowitz, H. (2011). Can Positive Thinking Be Negative? *Scientific American Mind*, *22*(2), 64–65. https://doi.org/10.1038/scientificamericanmind0511-64

Rodriguez, T. (2013). Taking the Bad with the Good. *Scientific American Mind*, *24*(2), 26–27. https://doi.org/10.1038/scientificamericanmind0513-26

Stokes, V. (2020, September 8). *Surprising Benefits of Negative Thinking*. Healthline; Healthline Media. https://www.healthline.com/health/positive-side-negative-thinking#takeaway

Stokes, V. (2020, September 8). *Surprising Benefits of Negative Thinking*. Healthline; Healthline Media. https://www.healthline.com/health/positive-side-negative-thinking#takeaway

positran_auriane. (2020, June 25). *the positive impact of negative emotions*. POSITRAN.

https://www.positran.eu/positive-impact-negative-emotions/

Andrews, P. W., & Thomson, J. A. (2009). The bright side of being blue: Depression as an adaptation for analyzing complex problems. *Psychological Review, 116*(3), 620–654. https://doi.org/10.1037/a0016242

Stokes, V. (2020, September 8). *Surprising Benefits of Negative Thinking.* Healthline; Healthline Media. https://www.healthline.com/health/positive-side-negative-thinking#takeaway

Bastian, B., & Humphrey, A. (2021, November 9). *What is toxic positivity and how does it impact happiness?* World Economic Forum. https://www.weforum.org/agenda/2021/11/how-to-avoid-toxic-positivity-happiness-mental-health/

Lilienfeld, S. O., & Arkowitz, H. (2011). Can Positive Thinking Be Negative? *Scientific American Mind, 22*(2), 64–65. https://doi.org/10.1038/scientificamericanmind0511-64

Lilienfeld, S. O., & Arkowitz, H. (2011). Can Positive Thinking Be Negative? *Scientific American Mind, 22*(2), 64–65. https://doi.org/10.1038/scientificamericanmind0511-64

Wood, J. V., Elaine Perunovic, W. Q., & Lee, J. W. (2009). Positive self-statements: Power for some, peril for others. *Psychological Science*, *20*(7), 860–866. https://doi.org/10.1111/j.1467-9280.2009.02370.x

Kato, H., Jena, A. B., & Tsugawa, Y. (2020). Patient mortality after surgery on the surgeon's birthday: an observational study. *BMJ*, m4381. https://doi.org/10.1136/bmj.m4381

Chapter 3: Not Happiness. Meaning is Important

Frankl, V. E., Goleman, D., & Franz Vesely. (2020). *Yes to life: in spite of everything*. Beacon Press.

Frankl, V. E., Goleman, D., & Franz Vesely. (2020). *Yes to life: in spite of everything*. Beacon Press.

Frankl, V. E., Goleman, D., & Franz Vesely. (2020). *Yes to life: in spite of everything*. Beacon Press.

Weir, K. (2020, April 1). Nurtured by Nature. *American Psychological Association*, *51*(3). https://www.apa.org/monitor/2020/04/nurtured-nature

Frankl, V. E., Goleman, D., & Franz Vesely. (2020). *Yes to life: in spite of everything*. Beacon Press.

Chapter 4: A Refreshing Look at Unwanted Things

1) Pink, D. H. (2022). *The power of regret: how looking backward moves us forward*. Riverhead Books.

Part 2

Chapter 7: What is an Emotion?

University of West Alabama. (2019, June 27). *The Science of Emotion: Exploring the Basics of Emotional Psychology | UWA Online*. UWA Online. https://online.uwa.edu/news/emotional-psychology/

Trauma | Psychology Today Canada. (n.d.). Www.psychologytoday.com. https://www.psychologytoday.com/ca/basics/trauma

Trauma | Psychology Today Canada. (n.d.). Www.psychologytoday.com. https://www.psychologytoday.com/ca/basics/trauma

Chapter 8: A Guide to Emotional Self-Regulation

Vallejo, M. (2023, December 6). *How to Process Emotions: A Step-by-Step Approach to Managing Emotions*. Mental Health Center Kids. https://mentalhealthcenterkids.com/blogs/articles/how-to-process-emotions

Listenburg, F. V. (2020). *Get to know yourself "3 uncomfortable Questions"*. Instagram. https://www.instagram.com/reel/C9AGa9CMo8v/?igsh=MWx4cmJ0aTY1ZTd0ag==

McAdam, E. (2024, March 21). *Window of Tolerance -An Essential Skill for PTSD, Trauma and Nervous System Regulation*. YouTube. https://youtu.be/PtDsHXXZjf4?si=UZ4Ux3ruoA5WC7Ru

Also by Avinash Sai:

Immature

Haunted by the Unknown: A collection of short stories

www.ingramcontent.com/pod-product-compliance
Lightning Source LLC
Chambersburg PA
CBHW062218150726
47991CB00006B/2339